THE COMPLETE GUIDE TO
NORTH AMERICAN
· GARDENS ·

VOLUME ONE

THE NORTHEAST

THE COMPLETE GUIDE TO
NORTH AMERICAN
· GARDENS ·

VOLUME ONE
THE NORTHEAST

WILLIAM C. MULLIGAN

FOREWORD BY LINDA YANG

Little, Brown and Company

Boston • Toronto • London

First Edition

THE COMPLETE GUIDE TO NORTH AMERICAN GARDENS
was conceived and produced by
Running Heads Incorporated
55 West 21 Street
New York, NY 10010

Editor: Charles A. de Kay
Designer: Liz Trovato
Managing Editor: Lindsey Crittenden
Production Manager: Linda Winters
Photo Editor: Ellie Watson
Photo Researcher: Tonia Smith

ISBN 0-316-58907-1
Library of Congress Catalog Card Number: 90-52886
Library of Congress Cataloging-in-Publication information is available.

10 9 8 7 6 5 4 3 2 1

Published simultaneously in Canada by Little, Brown & Company
(Canada) Limited

The photograph of the temple of love on page 14 is reproduced courtesy of Nemours Mansion and Gardens.

Typeset by Trufont Typographers, Inc.
Color separations by Hong Kong Scanner Craft Company Ltd.
Printed and bound in Singapore by Tien Wah Press (Pte.) Ltd.

ACKNOWLEDGMENTS

The comprehensive nature of this book is such that its development was in no way a single-handed endeavor. For its ultimate realization against sometimes daunting odds, I am enormously indebted to the Brooklyn Botanic Garden's Director Emeritus Elizabeth Scholtz and its Director of Publications Barbara Pesch, both of whom steered me in the right direction, lent encouragement when it was needed and alerted me to worthy gardens I might otherwise have overlooked. In this same regard, heartfelt thanks go to Elvin McDonald, Ann Lovejoy, Jerry Sedenko, Bob Lilly, Lynden Miller, Dr. Stephen Tim, Jacqueline Heriteau, Ken Druse, Sue Lathrop of The American Association of Botanic Gardens and Arboreta, and Linda Yang, whose foreword to this book and positive response to the manuscript at an early stage lifted my spirits immeasurably.

I thank all of the gardens contained herein for their enthusiastic cooperation in supplying information, materials, and photography, and I thank the late David Jacobson, my computer mentor, without whose encouragement and inspiration I never would have become "computerized," and would probably still be hacking away at an antiquated typewriter, much to the dismay of my editor. And he, Charles de Kay, deserves one of the biggest thanks of all for his limitless patience and valuable guidance.

Hugs, kisses, and thanks go to my friends and family members, without whose loyal encouragement and unfailing help in so many ways, this book would never have been written: Eleanor Mulligan, Pamala Hall, Dennis Hall, Carla Glasser, Lawrence Power, Lea Davies, Bonny and David Martin, Hope Hendler, Diane McMullen, Marie Iervolino, Rose and Joseph Kaht, Annette Perazzo, Linda Fox, and Janis Blackschleger.

CONTENTS

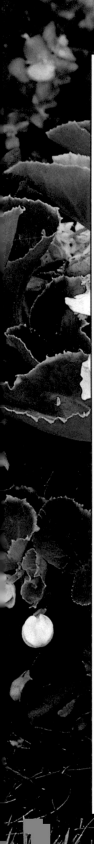

FOREWORD

It seems a millennium since that day in the early 1970s when a freckle-faced redhead named Bill Mulligan first came to poke around my city garden and discuss Serious Horticultural Subjects such as how I coped with aphids on my roses in a tiny plot in New York City.

At the time, Bill had already chosen to forgo his original career as a concert pianist, and with several garden articles to his credit, was working as co-editor of a gardening magazine. I was duly impressed with his deft queries, which I have since come to realize were merely his normal working style: a combination of careful study, research, lots of checking, and then lots more checking, again.

And indeed it is his track record of perseverance and careful journalism that leads me to believe that this series of garden guides will provide precisely the beacon that every weary traveler needs.

The idea of trekking through North American public gardens—which includes assorted former private estates as well as arboretums and botanical gardens—is a relatively recent phenomenon. Unlike the British, we have no history of national "open-today" gardens. Neither can we boast sites as ancient as Hadrian's estate near Rome, which dates from 138 A.D., or vistas as grand as Le Nôtre's mile-long perspective at Versailles.

But in this vast space between the Atlantic and Pacific we are blessed with a diversity of climate, topography, and soil, and just enough centuries of horticultural influences to have inspired a certain independence—some might even say eccentricity—of landscape thought and design.

It no longer surprises to hear that Americans have an increased interest in gardening. Even the most casual of green thumbs now studies those perfectly pruned and groomed plants in public landscapes with an occasional twinge of envy. Indeed it is quickly becoming routine to leave our own weeding and watering chores behind and submit to miles of detours (whether by air, land, or sea) for the pure exhilaration of strolling past intoxicatingly fragrant herbs, exploring woodsy trails edged with unfamiliar wildflowers, or standing in mute deference before an ancient bonsai.

Which still leaves the problem of unearthing these horticultural gems in the first place. For they are just as likely to be hidden within a Massachusetts suburb (such as that which surrounds the Garden in the Woods) as tucked into a mountain-rimmed Pacific peninsula (the breathtaking backdrop for the Botanical Garden of the University of British Columbia).

Helpful garden guides abound on other sides of the seas, but New World explorers have largely been forced to make do with tour books geared to general consumption—wherein is found little solace for the horticulturally inclined. To the rescue at last come these handsome guides, which are also conveniently sized not only for zipping in and out of underseat luggage but for tossing onto a dashboard.

The books are organized into two major sections. The first, which is comfortably readable without distractions, begins by setting the scene with state maps for quick pinpointing of each garden's place. This is followed by Bill's concise essays of that area's significant sites.

Highlighted in these hundred or so compositions is a personal, somewhat eclectic, assortment of subjects, chosen for what Bill believed would be each garden's primary interest to visitors. You feel he's right there, beside you, providing gentle guidance. In addition to the one or more specialized plant collections of note, other particulars range from aspects of the garden's history, its outstanding architectural features, design or stylistic influences, the primary season of interest, and portraits of founders, former owners, or present supporters.

The essays, along with the color photographs, are a superb introduction to these gardens and invaluable not only for excursion plotting and planning but for sedentary armchair dreams.

The latter portion of the book neatly enumerates the nitty-gritty facts. Here are all the essentials required for visiting each place, with directions, addresses, phone numbers, hours, and admission policies. This host of indispensables in capsule form also includes information on varied related activities such as workshops, children's attractions, and library use. Included are symbols delineating the existence of plant labels, guided tours, visitor centers, gift shops, and courses.

Despite the plethora of information these books contain, the perceptive reader sooner or later will note Bill's distinctly nonjudgmental mien—an approach for which I, for one, am grateful. Notwithstanding most gardeners' predilection for voicing strong personal opinions, it is only misleading to attempt to compare a continent of landscapes whose scope encompasses the moody and mysterious as well as the fastidiously restored. It is patently unfair, if not downright impossible, to pronounce equivalents between, for example, the nineteenth-century specimen trees on an elegant former estate (like the Morris Arboretum of the University of Pennsylvania) and the merry kaleidoscope of bedding species (found at Butchart Gardens in Victoria, on Canada's westernmost coast).

On the other hand, it is only natural, if after surveying these glorious gardens, you find yourself trying to determine which, in fact, is Bill's preferred place to linger. Or maybe mine.

However, you're going to have to pick a favorite spot for yourself. Because I'll never tell. And—being a proper reporter—neither will he.

—Linda Yang
New York City

INTRODUCTION

It was my objective in preparing this book not only to illuminate beautiful gardens and to encourage interested travelers to experience their enchanting color and fragrance firsthand, but also to make the reader aware of the increasingly important role these institutions play with regard to ecological and environmental concerns and conservation of endangered species. Information, advice, encouragement, and a sympathetic ear are waiting at many of them for anyone willing to seek them out. At a time of critical threat to the world's ecosystems and overall health of the planet itself, the significance of these organizations grows by leaps and bounds. Their efforts deserve support, and the majority invite membership, for which privileges are granted in return.

The histories of these gardens reflect the history of America itself, its hopes, its dreams, its moral responsibility. Whether a research facility, a university-associated arboretum, an amusement park, a restored private estate, a community park, or a scientifically oriented botanic garden, each invariably represents the passion and vision of a single individual or group determined to create something beautiful and to improve our world in the process.

Read as a whole, this work will reveal certain trends, personal pursuits, and changes in our society. It also supplies much in the way of gardening information and inspiration. But it is still a travel guide, arranged for convenient reference. All of the gardens are listed alphabetically by state and city. The front of the book offers descriptive essays and color photographs of the gardens, while the back contains ready-reference, essential information regarding addresses and telephone numbers, travel directions, hours open, admission-fee policies, degrees of wheelchair accessibility, and special features, such as zoos or museums. Symbols, with a key to their meanings, indicate the presence at each garden of such amenities as a gift shop, plant labeling, a restaurant, parking areas, and availability of courses and membership.

Armchair ruminations are fine. Inspiration from the printed word and the beauty of a well-taken picture are always welcome. But travel the highways and byways and experience nature's boundless beauty and mystery for yourself. There is no substitute.

—William C. Mulligan
New York City

THE UNITED STATES

CONNECTICUT

HARTFORD

NEW LONDON

STAMFORD

CONNECTICUT COLLEGE ARBORETUM
New London

A long path lined with mountain laurel and red cedar forms an appropriately impressive main entrance to this 425-acre repository of nature's bounty. Surrounding the Connecticut College campus and administered by the Botany Department, the arboretum was established in 1931 to provide students and the public with research in horticulture, conservation, and ecology. Its forests, wetlands, and fields concentrate on displays of trees and shrubs native to eastern North America and hardy in New London.

Over 300 kinds of woody plants are cultivated, and seasonal interest continues throughout the year: shadbush in April; dogwood and azaleas in May; mountain laurel in June; giant rhododendron, sourwood, and sweet pepperbush in July; striking autumn foliage in October; and evergreens and conifers year-round. Major attractions include the collections of heaths and viburnums, The Lillian Dauby Gries Conifer Collection, The Edgerton and Stengel Wildflower Gardens, and The Caroline Black Garden. This last, named after the member of the Botany Department who designed it in 1921, is a four-acre contoured landscape with unusual, mature specimens of flowering trees and shrubs.

Mountain laurel is a June attraction at the Connecticut College Arboretum.

BARTLETT ARBORETUM
Stamford

Occupying 63 sylvan acres of the Connecticut countryside, the Bartlett Arboretum is associated with the Department of Plant Sciences, College of Agriculture and Natural Resources, of The University of Connecticut. An outstanding feature of this marvelous, expansive preserve is the organization of its nature trails, each designed to acquaint the visitor, or student, with a particular kind of plant or ecological system. The Woodland Trail,

Cherry blossoms are harbingers of spring at Bartlett Arboretum.

for example, wanders through a natural forest containing such native trees as maples, oaks, dogwoods, beeches, alders, and birches. Along Swamp Walk, an elevated footbridge encourages visitors to appreciate the wonders of a natural wetland, abounding with marsh marigolds, cardinal flowers, violets, and ferns, not to mention jack-in-the-pulpit and skunk cabbage. Needle Evergreen Walk invites inspection of various pines, spruces, firs, hemlocks, true cedars, and a variety of cultivars of false cypress.

A garden of slow-growing and dwarf conifers of all kinds and an extensive ericaceous collection reflect the arboretum's emphasis on these two areas. The latter includes both a stand of native rhododendrons and azaleas and a garden of named varieties and hybrids of these glorious bloomers from Japan, Korea, and Europe. Both the conifer and ericaceous gardens familiarize the homeowner and professional landscaper with the kinds that perform well in the Connecticut area. Equally edifying and inspiring are the arboretum's collections of nut trees (pecan, walnut, heartnut, Bartlett chestnut, among others), daffodils (in early spring), and pollarded trees, offering the results of special pruning techniques.

The arboretum's living collection had its beginning in 1913 when Dr. Francis A. Bartlett, an eminent dendrologist (tree and shrub expert), acquired "30 acres more or less" of woodland for experimental and research purposes. The site became Dr. Bartlett's residence, as well, and he planted it with a number of species from all over the world. By 1965 the tract had increased to its present size, and through the efforts of a citizen group called the Bartlett Arboretum Association, it was purchased that year by the state and annexed to The University of Connecticut.

DELAWARE

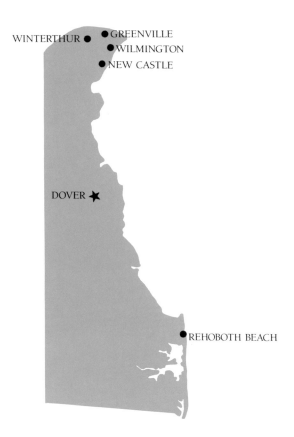

WINTERTHUR ● ● GREENVILLE
● WILMINGTON
● NEW CASTLE

DOVER ★

● REHOBOTH BEACH

MT. CUBA CENTER FOR THE STUDY OF PIEDMONT FLORA
Greenville

Designed and owned by Mrs. Lammot du Pont Copeland, the beautifully naturalized landscape of Mt. Cuba Center has been under development since the 1960s. Beginning in 1985, Mrs. Copeland has opened the site to the public on a limited basis during the spring months, when its mountain laurel, flowering trees, wildflowers, and native rhododendrons are in peak bloom. Indigenous trees and shrubs, ponds, woodlands, meadows, and hillsides complemented by the introduced cultivated species of an expert collector make this a rare and delightful garden to investigate.

The springtime bloom of mountain laurel draws visitors to Mt. Cuba Center.

THE GEORGE READ II HOUSE AND GARDEN
New Castle

Recognized only recently for their unique historical significance, the gardens of this magnificent eighteenth-century mansion are the focus of methodical restoration efforts at this writing. Designed by Robert and David Buist of Philadelphia and installed in 1847–1848, the landscape—in the style of Andrew Jackson Downing (see Lyndhurst, Tarrytown, New York, p. 87)—continues to flaunt many of its original trees and 90 percent of its seminal design. Extensive photography done in the 1870s and 1880s substantiates the present-day garden's impeccable pedigree. Spring bulb flowers, specimen trees and shrubs, and formal beds outlined with boxwood are some of the features awaiting visitors to this charming nineteenth-century setting.

The clean-lined symmetry and grace of the exterior and interior of the manor house, under construction between 1797 and 1804, represent the epitome of Federal fashion. Built for George Read, a prominent lawyer and son of a signer of the Declaration of Independence and the Constitution, the house is located in historic New Castle, a well-preserved colonial village of cobblestone streets, spacious greenswards, and period buildings. It was the second owner of the homestead, William Couper, who commissioned the gardens that survive today and that were featured in the October 1901 issue of *House and Garden* magazine. The final residents of Read House, Mr. and Mrs. Philip D. Laird, acquired the property in 1902. Upon the death of Mrs. Laird in 1975, it was bequeathed to the Historical Society of Delaware, which has since overseen its preservation and maintenance.

Elegant formal gardens are a highlight of The George Read II House.

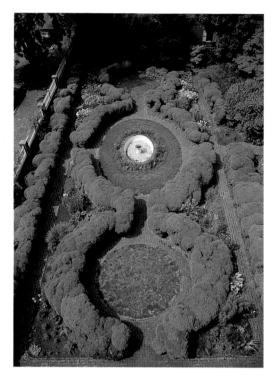

THE HOMESTEAD
Rehoboth Beach

Owned and maintained by the Rehoboth Art League, Inc., The Homestead, dating from 1743 and listed in the National Register of Historic Places, is the oldest estate in Rehoboth Beach. An impressive manor house stands guard over five eighteenth-century–style formal gardens, established in 1938, each outlined with clipped English boxwood (*Buxus sempervirens* 'Suffruticosa'). Commemorating the coronation of Elizabeth II, the Crown Garden is planted with columbine, foxglove, and begonias. The Chain Garden features roses and an abundant variety of sedums. A broad selection of medicinal and culinary herbs distinguishes the Herb Garden. The Criss-Cross Garden, undergoing restoration at this writing, is a show of bulb flowers hovering over a variety of groundcovers. The Tea Terrace, with a millstone table and carved cedar seats, presents a genteel setting for relaxation and contemplation.

The grounds encompass the Corkran Tubbs Galleries and facilities for the Art League's studios and classrooms. Other features of interest include a gazebo, the Sundial Garden, and the Drying Yard, with a concord grape arbor and fig trees. Flourishing in various areas throughout the property are hydrangeas, cotoneasters, forsythias, pachysandra, vinca, ajuga, spirea, ivy varieties, and a specimen kousa dogwood.

Begonia semperflorens *is among* The Homestead's *summer bedding plants.*

ELEUTHERIAN MILLS
Wilmington

Eleuthère Irénée (E. I.) du Pont came to America in 1800 with the dream of finding his fortune. He did just that on the shores of the picturesque Brandywine River, establishing first a gunpowder mill and later a textile plant. For his wife and seven children, he built a homestead that grew to reflect the expanding prosperity of his enterprises. Beginning in 1803, true to the heritage of his native country where he had gardened in his youth, du Pont laid out a kitchen garden in the French style, formally geometric and combining ornamentals with edibles. To derive the most from limited growing space, the French had become masters of training, or espaliering, fruit trees, and du Pont adopted the demanding, exacting practice for his American property. Today, the garden at Eleutherian Mills is a showplace of this almost-lost horticultural art form in all its manifestations: pear trees with branches trained downward to form tent shapes (*en quenouille*), upward into fan shapes and crisscrossed diamond-lattice style into a form known as a Belgian fence; a pleached allee, two rows of lady apple trees, their uppermost branches curved over and worked together to form a long, tunnel-like archway over a gravel path; and lines of apple trees pruned so severely that only low branches trained horizontally remain, forming two-foot-high fences (*cordons*).

The two-acre garden was restored in 1972 by landscape architect William H. Frederick according to archaeological excavations that had commenced in 1968. Du Pont imported seeds and cuttings from the Jardin des Plantes in Paris, and is said to have introduced the poppy (*Papaver orientale*) to America. The garden's spring show of bulbs, dogwoods, magnolias, lilacs, and azaleas, and summer parade of roses, sunflowers, dahlias, marigolds, nasturtiums, zinnias, and lobelia reflect du Pont's recorded choices, wherever possible. In the vegetable garden, violets, primulas, and buttercups grow charmingly cheek by jowl with onions, lettuce, and asparagus.

The Georgian-style mansion at Eleutherian Mills is filled with art and furnishings accumulated by the five generations of du Ponts who lived there. Also contained within the estate complex are: a barn with carriages, wagons, and vintage automobiles; a cooper's shop; the Du Pont Company's first office building; a latticed gazebo; and an Italianate garden, inspired by the Villa d'Este and built in the 1920s by Irénée's great-granddaughter, Louise Crowninshield, complete with colonnades, statuary, and manufac-

The restored kitchen garden (ca. 1803) at Eleutherian Mills.

Formal gardens aligned along an axis exalt the mansion at Nemours.

tured "ruins." The Hagley Museum, of which Eleutherian Mills is but a part, is a 230-acre National Historic Landmark offering a diversity of restorations, exhibits, and live demonstrations that present a glimpse of American life at home and at work in the early nineteenth century.

NEMOURS MANSION AND GARDENS
Wilmington

A little of the sublime, elegant majesty of Versailles found its way to America in the form of the Alfred I. du Pont estate, Nemours, named after the site of the du Pont ancestral home in France. The 102-room, pink stucco mansion, built in 1909–1910, was designed by Carrère & Hastings of New York in Louis XVI château style to preside over 300 acres of woodlands and magnificent formal gardens.

Completed in 1932 and entirely restored in recent years, the gardens were executed in the formal French manner, with elaborate fountains, parterre beds, allees, topiaries, and clipped hedges. Aligned along an axis that extends away from the mansion for a third of a mile and revealing their splendor in succession to the visitor are: the Vista, lined with Japanese cryptomeria, pink flowering horse chestnuts and pin oaks; the Maze Garden, its ornate Persian-carpet design delineated by hedges of Canadian hemlock and Helleri holly; the Colonnade, an awe-inspiring gallery transecting the axis, made of Indiana limestone and designed in 1926 by Stewart and Donahue of Wilmington as a memorial to Pierre Samuel du Pont de Nemours and his son Eleuthère Irénée du Pont (see Eleutherian Mills, p. 23); the Sunken Gardens, featuring a double grand staircase, an Italianate grotto, and a collection of bronze and marble statuary; and demanding admiration at the end of the axis, a classically styled temple of love, this one sheltering a life-size statue of Diana the Huntress cast by Jean Antoine Houdon (1741–1828).

The Southern Gardens, extending from the south side of the mansion to a wooded area, include three distinct designs: the Boxwood Garden, a French parterre executed in English boxwood (*Buxus sempervirens* 'Suffruticosa'); the Four Borders, named for its mixed herbaceous borders, encompassing 8,500 square feet of annuals and perennials; and the Frog Pond, softening the transition between the ornamental gardens and the woodland. A rock garden typical of those popular in nineteenth-century England, containing bulbs and dwarf conifers, and the Wren's Nest, a little gray playhouse used by the children of the manor, are two more of the grounds' many captivating features.

The rooms of the house contain fine examples of antique furniture, Oriental rugs, tapestries, and paintings dating back to the fifteenth century. Other vestiges of the du Ponts' opulent life-style on view are vintage automobiles, a billiard room, a ninepins alley, and a bottling room.

Spring narcissus add zest to the Rockwood Museum's Gardenesque grandeur.

ROCKWOOD MUSEUM
Wilmington

The country estate of Rockwood is a surviving example of nineteenth-century Rural Gothic architecture and Gardenesque ("natural") landscaping. Designed in 1851 by English architect George Williams for merchant banker Joseph Shipley, the estate includes a manor house with attached conservatory (winter garden), porter's lodge, gardener's cottage, and carriage house on 70 of its original 200 acres. Interior furnishings include seventeenth-, eighteenth-, and nineteenth-century decorative arts reflecting the tastes of a succession of family members.

The parklike setting of the grounds is typical of the Gardenesque approach to landscape design, popular in England in the mid-1800s and becoming fashionable in the United States a bit later. Definitive elements included large expanses of lawn interrupted by overgrown trees and shrubs, their placement not appearing too planned, and gently curving paths. In an age of increasing industrialization, landowners looked to their landscapes to remind them of nature's tranquil disorder. A leisurely stroll through the estate's grounds affords appreciation of its wonderful old trees, including a weeping beech (*Fagus sylvatica* 'Pendula') planted by Joseph Shipley around 1856, a sugar maple (*Acer saccharum*), a maidenhair tree (*Ginkgo biloba*) and a European larch (*Larix decidua*). Also to be found are nearly 100-year-old boxwood hedges and yew shrubs.

Listed in the National Register of Historic Places, the estate was acquired by New Castle County in 1972 through the bequest of Nancy Sellers Hargraves, a great-great-grandniece of Joseph Shipley. The museum and grounds are administered by the county's Department of Parks and Recreation.

WINTERTHUR MUSEUM AND GARDENS
Winterthur

The magnificent Winterthur, named for a town in Switzerland, was built in the late 1920s by Henry Francis du Pont, a cousin of the builders of Nemours (see p. 25) and Longwood (see p. 91) and great grandson of E. I. du Pont, the creator of Eleutherian Mills (see p. 23). Continuing in the tradition of this prodigious industrial and horticultural family, Henry Francis sought to preserve the natural beauty of the rolling hills and woodlands of his 1,000-acre estate. With the help of the Arnold Arboretum (see p. 37), he set about embellishing one-fifth of the acreage with various Oriental woody species, especially rhododendrons and azaleas of every hue and variety. Today, the grounds are alive with color in spring, especially in May when drifts of bulb flowers complement the vivid shades of the shrub blossoms. Annual color throughout the summer is offered by Oak Hill and March Bank, and fall color is supplied by berries, foliage, and asters. The Pinetum, with more than 50 species of rare conifers, comprises one of the most outstanding collections in America.

Housed in the estate's manor house, the Winterthur Museum presents a spectacular assemblage of seventeenth- to nineteenth-century art and decorative objects. Regularly scheduled 45-minute tram tours of the grounds make all of its varied and fascinating features easily accessible. The estate maintains a conservation program of propagating and distributing rare and endangered plants, and offers courses and workshops focused on its gardens and art collections.

Bulbs and flowering trees framing Winterthur's vast acreage in spring.

MAINE

WILD GARDENS OF ACADIA
Bar Harbor

A project of The Bar Harbor Garden Club, this three-quarter acre installation was established "to display, preserve and propagate the native flora of Maine's Mount Desert Island." Recognizing the unique combination of both cold- and warm-climate plants naturally present on the island, Charles W. Eliot and George B. Dorr began purchasing land in the early 1900s to be preserved for public enjoyment and scientific and educational purposes. The Sieur de Monts Spring area was acquired in 1909, and through a petition to the Federal Government, it was eventually declared Acadia National Park. When the Bar Harbor Garden Club was considering

Sensitive fern and white forget-me-nots civilize Acadia's Wild Gardens.

a planting of native wildflowers in 1961, space was offered at Sieur de Monts. Accepting the proposal, the garden club began clearing and planting, and named the results of their labors Wild Gardens of Acadia.

In the span of time since the early 1960s, more than 400 native species of ferns, heaths, wildflowers (one of the most outstanding displays in the country), and berries have been planted in areas simulating their natural habitats: mountain, meadow, roadside, bog, marsh, pond, beach, thicket, and woodland. An abundance of fascinating flowers and fruits may be found throughout the habitats from May through October. The gardens are operated by the Bar Harbor Garden Club with the help of the park, which maintains the water system and supplies plant labels, among other services.

MERRYSPRING
Camden

Astride the border dividing Camden and Rockport, Maine, sits a 66-acre natural preserve established "for the promotion, recognition, appreciation, and cultivation" of the state's indigenous plant life. Selected in 1974 by noted horticulturist Mary Ellen Ross as an ideal setting for the study of native flora, Merryspring strives to encourage appreciation of both the rare and familiar among these treasures and to show how they may be cultivated and preserved.

The exhilarating pastoral environment encompasses a number of varied landscapes experienced via a system of trails. These include the 10-acre Kitty Todd Arboretum, herb and lily gardens, raised beds, the Margaret Taylor Pattison Woodlands garden, and demonstration gardens of all kinds supplying ideas for homeowners. Native wildflowers, wild strawberries, ferns, evergreen ground covers, fragrant shrubs such as bayberry and sweetfern, stands of hop-hornbeam and white pine, all kinds of wildlife, and scenic views of the surrounding countryside are just some of the wonders in store for visitors to this northeastern coastal microcosm.

Offering a variety of exhibitions, workshops, and special events throughout the year, Merryspring is a nonprofit corporation sustained by contributions and memberships.

Native meadow flowers account for some of the allure of Merryspring.

DEERING OAKS ROSE CIRCLE
Portland

Awaiting discovery within sprawling, 50-acre Deering Oaks Park is a charming one-acre rose garden-in-the-round. Displaying 700 bushes encompassing 31 varieties of floribundas and hybrid teas, this official All-America Rose Selections test garden is best appreciated when in peak bloom, during the months of June through August. Great old shade trees and expanses of lawn in the surrounding park invite leisurely strolls and relaxed picnicking.

Large-flower hybrids like 'Typhoon' scent the air at Deering Oaks Rose Circle.

Oriental poppies are among Hamilton House's old-fashioned favorites.

HAMILTON HOUSE
South Berwick

Like a ghostly mirage from the past, the elegantly austere all-white Hamilton House rises atop a bluff overlooking the Piscataqua River. Its history reflects the local prevailing industry's shift over the years from timber trade and shipping to farming. When the 1785 house's builder, Col. Jonathan Hamilton, lost his fortune as a result of the shipping embargoes of the War of 1812, he was forced to sell his 300-acre estate. It flourished as a sheep farm from 1839 until 1898, when the decline of the agricultural economy prompted its sale once again.

Sarah Orne Jewett, famous for her stories of country life in Maine, was enamored of the house, having visited it frequently as a child and having borrowed it as the setting for one of her romantic novels, *The Tory Lover.* Concerned that the structure would fall into ruin, she persuaded Mrs. Emily Tyson to purchase it. This generous patron set out to restore the house as it might have appeared during Col. Hamilton's ownership. She planted old-fashioned trees and shrubs and established a Colonial formal garden with a pergola and an adjacent summerhouse made from fragments of a ruined saltbox.

Through the bequest of Mrs. Tyson's daughter, Mrs. Henry Vaughan, the house and its grounds have been shared with the public since 1949. Recently refurbished, the gardens today reflect Mrs. Tyson's legacy of traditional plantings laid out in symmetrical beds. Her gracious formal garden, centering on a sundial, features boxwood-lined flower beds and is surrounded by manicured hedges. Rolling lawn, stately old trees, and flower-lined paths complete the old-world ambience.

Adjacent to the property, Vaughan Woods Memorial State Park offers nature trails, picnic areas, and a sublime view of Hamilton House. The estate is owned and operated by The Society for the Preservation of New England Antiquities, a nonprofit organization supported by federal and state agencies, private donations, and membership enrollment.

MASSACHUSETTS

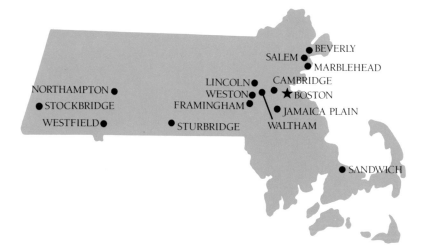

NORTHAMPTON ●
● STOCKBRIDGE
WESTFIELD ●

LINCOLN ●
WESTON ●
FRAMINGHAM ●
● STURBRIDGE

SALEM ● ● BEVERLY
● MARBLEHEAD
CAMBRIDGE
● ★ BOSTON
● JAMAICA PLAIN
WALTHAM

● SANDWICH

SEDGWICK GARDENS AT LONG HILL
Beverly

In 1916 Ellery Sedgwick, a successful author and the editor of the *Atlantic Monthly*, and his wife, Mabel Cabot Sedgwick, purchased 114 acres of pastureland with panoramic views of the surrounding countryside. They built a mansion that was a copy of the Isaac Ball House (1802) in Charleston, South Carolina, appropriating the original's interior wood carvings and shipping them to the site. Mrs. Sedgwick, herself the author of *The Garden Month by Month* (1907) and an avid horticulturist, installed lavish gardens that combined native cedar with mountain laurel, Japanese weeping cherries, lilacs, roses, a wide variety of azaleas, and carpets of scillas, snowdrops, and chionodoxas.

After her death in 1937, the grounds inherited the attentions of another distinguished caretaker, the former Marjorie Russell of England, a propagator of rare plants and the second Mrs. Sedgwick. To ensure continual summer-through-fall flowering and vivid foliage color in autumn, she consulted with the celebrated Arnold Arboretum (see p. 37) and added an exceptional collection of tree peonies, koelreuterias, oxydendrums, sophora, stewartias, lotuses, and Japanese maples. The gardens today, containing 400 species, remain as a tribute to the knowledge and devotion of these two extraordinary women.

Dispersed among features that number a cutting garden, rose and grape arbors, lotus and lily pools, a Chinese gate, fences and pagoda, an ironwork pavilion from France, and a gray garden, major collections include rhododendrons, hostas, tree peonies, dogwoods, cherries, and crab apples.

In 1979 Ellery Sedgwick's four children gave Long Hill to The Trustees of Reservations, a nonprofit organization that operates and maintains 71 historic homes (see Naumkeag, p. 43) throughout Massachusetts. An endowment for the ongoing maintenance of Long Hill was provided at the bequest of Marjorie Sedgwick, and the North Shore Garden Club continues to offer advice and assistance regarding the preservation of the gardens.

Azaleas were a love of Mabel Sedgwick, Long Hill's first mistress.

ISABELLA STEWART GARDNER MUSEUM
Boston

This jewel of an art institution is the remarkable achievement of Isabella Stewart Gardner, who amassed the collection, designed the building, and endowed it for posterity. As the bride of John L. Gardner in 1860, this prominent member of Boston society began collecting books, manuscripts, sculpture, textiles, furniture, ceramics, and metalwork, and with her husband, formed one of the first great collections of old master paintings in America. A widow by the turn of the century, Mrs. Gardner built Fenway Court, designing it in the style of a fifteenth-century Venetian palace, to house acquisitions that numbered over 2,000, from cultures spanning more than 30 centuries. Fenway Court and its magnificent collection were officially opened to the public in 1903. Mrs. Gardner occupied an apartment in the building until her death in 1924.

The light-filled, atrium-like courtyard at the heart of the museum reflects Mrs. Gardner's passion for Italianate gardens, as well as objects. Towering palms, plantings of myrtle, bay, pomegranate, olive, a variety of citrus trees, and classical statuary all pay homage to a second-century Roman mosaic floor laid in the center of the garden. Displays of potted seasonal flowers, changed each Easter (cineraria, lilies), spring (azaleas), fall (begonias, chrysanthemums) and Christmas (poinsettias), keep the courtyard alive with color.

Outside the building, the South Garden, also formal in character and redesigned in 1977 by Eleanor M. McPeck, features an allee of Japanese katsura trees, and star magnolias softly framing a statue of Diana. A more informal garden of woody plants, called the Monks' Garden, lies just outside the building, to the east.

Abiding by Mrs. Gardner's will, the Isabella Stewart Gardner Museum, Inc., was established in 1936 to ensure the preservation of her collection "for the education and enjoyment of the public forever." In the many decades since then, successive generations of trustees and staff have carried on the founder's mandate.

Seasonal flowers bask in the light of the Gardner Museum's central court.

LONGFELLOW NATIONAL HISTORIC SITE
Cambridge

Home to America's beloved poet from 1837 to 1882 and the place where he penned his most famous works, this historic house remains today as it was in Longfellow's lifetime, filled with his furniture and cherished possessions. The extraordinary example of eighteenth-century Georgian architecture was built in 1759 and expanded in 1793. It was a gift in 1843 to the celebrated writer, who had been a lodger in the house, and his new wife, Fanny, from the bride's father, Nathan Appleton. Years earlier, the ubiquitous George Washington had chosen the house as his headquarters during the siege of Boston, and he and Martha celebrated their seventeenth anniversary in it in January of 1776. The inviting 1½-acre garden, preserved exactly as Longfellow himself had originally planned it, is an agreeable combination of large old trees, open lawn, stands of flowering shrubs, and formal beds of perennials and annuals bordered by boxwood. A pleasingly proportioned trellis-covered seat backed by a wall of latticework adds to the garden's old-world graciousness. The mansion and grounds are maintained by the National Park Service of the U.S. Department of the Interior, to which they were donated in 1973.

Boxwood-bordered beds stocked with perennials and annuals grace Longfellow.

MOUNT AUBURN CEMETERY
Cambridge

As America's first cemetery conceived as a garden, Mount Auburn inspired similar installations throughout the country. Founded in 1831 by a group belonging to the Massachusetts Horticultural Society, it became independent of that organization in 1835 under the leadership of Dr. Jacob Bigelow, the designer, among others, of the original grounds and the cemetery's president for over 25 years. The 172 acres of scrupulously manicured lawns and ornamental plantings serve as the final resting place for a number of famous Americans, including Henry Wadsworth Longfellow, Oliver Wendell Holmes, Winslow Homer, Edwin Booth, Mary Baker Eddy, R. Buckminster Fuller, and Asa Gray.

Elaborate Victorian and Greek-temple inspired monuments adorn sweeping vistas every bit as effectively as well-sited garden architecture. Several embody the work of the country's most celebrated sculptors, among them Augustus Saint-Gaudens whose New Hampshire homestead is a National Historic Site (see p. 48). An intimate garden in memory of nineteenth-century botanist and taxonomist Asa Gray is a tribute in spring to blooming dogwood, Japanese cherries, and azaleas. It is the artful placement of the trees and shrubs, in fact, that accounts for the elegant beauty of Mount Auburn's landscape. From stately maples to flowering ornamentals, more than 5,000 specimens encompass over 580 different species. Complementing these every summer are some 30,000 annuals tucked into 600 small and 20 more sizable beds. Other noteworthy features of the cemetery are a 60 foot tower with a panoramic view of Boston, two chapels, one built in 1845, the other in 1898, and an antique, Egyptian-motif gate.

Mount Auburn glows with breathtaking tree and shrub bloom in spring.

GARDEN IN THE WOODS
Framingham

Perhaps the loveliest naturalistic setting in the Northeast and without a doubt its largest landscaped collection of wildflowers, the 45-acre Garden in the Woods flourishes with more than 1,500 varieties, including 200 kinds that are rare nationally, regionally, or locally. A walk along its three miles of trails is guaranteed to renew the spirit and boggle the mind at the richness and diversity of nature's bounty. A woodland sanctuary occupies 30 of the acres, while 15 are devoted to a series of specially designed gardens: Sunny Bog, Meadow, Lily Pond, Rhododendron Grove, Brookside, and Lady's-Slipper Paths.

Beginning in early spring and continuing through late fall, shrubs, trees, and wildflowers radiate uninterrupted bloom: soft-hued, fragile hepaticas, trailing arbutus, and golden marsh marigolds in April; yellow lady's slippers, trilliums, and carpets of woodland phlox in May; flame azaleas, mountain laurels, rhododendrons, prickly pear cacti (including a native New England variety), and pitcher plants in June; Turk's-cap lilies and blazing stars in July; butterflies darting among coneflowers, black-eyed Susans, red cardinal flowers, and turtleheads in August; and blue gentians and New England asters in September and October.

Since 1965, the garden has been owned by the New England Wild Flower Society, a leading proponent of native-plant conservation from the time it was founded in 1922. The installation's creation in the 1930s and much of its development is credited to W. C. Curtis and H. O. Stiles, two men whose devotion to searching out rare and exotic plants resulted in one of the best wildflower gardens in North America. Continuing that legacy, the society researches new propagation techniques, encourages home-owners to grow wildflowers by making plants and seeds available, and publishes a newsletter, magazine, and a selection of booklets. As a not-for-profit educational organization, it is funded by an endowment, grants, and private contributions.

Bloodroot casts its unique spell among the wildflowers that account for the Garden in the Woods.

The Arnold Arboretum is a place of rare beauty, even in early winter.

THE ARNOLD ARBORETUM OF HARVARD UNIVERSITY
Jamaica Plain

The 265 acres of the Arnold Arboretum's Living Plant Collections in Jamaica Plain encompass "the oldest arboretum in North America intended for both university and public use." The university in this case is no less than Harvard, located in nearby Cambridge. And offered by this august institution to the public at large is a parklike setting of hills and dells planted with more than 7,000 different kinds of trees, shrubs, and vines.

Established in 1872 and named for its benefactor, James Arnold, the installation was planned and designed by Charles Sprague Sargent, its first director, and the celebrated architect of the American landscape, Frederick Law Olmsted. The varied collection of rare woody specimens found throughout the Arnold is representative of the more than 2,000 plants the arboretum plant explorers, notably Chinese Wilson, have introduced to North American gardens.

On a visit in early winter, I was especially taken with the grounds' scenic vistas, including a view, from the highest point, of the Boston skyline some miles away. Among the plant features that attracted my attention were the pure-white bare stems of *Rubus lasiostylus*, the intricate bark patterns of a paperbark maple, and the delicate pinkish seedheads of *Heptacodium jasminoides*, all of which would be excellent candidates for landscaping in the Northeast, specifically for creating winter interest. Additional noteworthy features include a renowned collection of lilacs, the Larz Anderson Bonsai Collection, and the Bradley Collection of plants of the Rose Family.

Water lilies participate in Codman House's summer-flower performance.

CODMAN HOUSE, THE GRANGE
Lincoln

Its elegant symmetry sited on a knoll and commanding views of the surrounding gardens and countryside, the Codman House was built during the years 1735 to 1741 by the politically prominent Russell family. In 1790 ownership passed to merchant John Codman, a relative who made additions that more than doubled the house's size, importing skilled woodcarvers and plasterers from Boston to bedeck the manse with ornament of the highest quality. As lord of the manor in 1862, his son, Ogden Codman, Sr., commissioned architect John Hubbard Sturgis to make further alterations, this time in the fashion of the Victorian period. Later in the same century, Ogden Codman, Jr., who was to become a designer to the wealthy of Boston and New York (see Newport Mansions, p. 101), left his own mark on the house by installing the second-story bedrooms with Colonial-Revival paneling and laying out the grounds' Italianate garden. The house as it stands today, reflecting the interests of its successive owners, is a fascinating amalgam of elements from Georgian, Federal, Victorian, and Colonial-Revival periods, all overlaid with the decorative musing of neoclassical architect and latticework designer, Ogden Codman, Jr.

As befitting a country estate laid out in the English manner, the grounds' splendid parklike setting is filled with specimen trees, flower gardens, a rare example of a ha-ha, or sunken barrier, and the beguiling Italianate garden, with terraces, fountains, statuary, and a reflecting pool stocked with water lilies. The house and gardens are owned and maintained by The Society for the Preservation of New England Antiquities, a nonprofit organization that welcomes membership.

Lilacs' spring scent perfumes Lee Mansion.

JEREMIAH LEE MANSION
Marblehead

Regarded by some as one of the finest Georgian structures in America, this imposing three-story stone edifice was built in 1768 for Col. Jeremiah Lee and his wife, Martha. No doubt the prosperous Colonel Lee would have had a garden befitting the splendor of his house, but since no information about it has ever been found, the Marblehead Garden Club's restoration efforts over the years have been the result of meticulous detective work. Studying eighteenth-century gardens throughout New England and conducting research at the Massachusetts Horticultural Society, The Society for the Preservation of New England Antiquities, and other institutions and sources, the club has created a garden that is as historically accurate as possible in terms of design and plant materials.

Pervaded by a soothing formal ambience, the finished product includes a Sundial Garden, with serpentine beds encircling an ornamental timepiece appropriate to the period, a geometrically laid-out herb garden planted with more than 30 kinds, an abundantly stocked perennial garden, and a sunken garden dominated by an expanse of lawn and bordered by trees, shrubs, and 26 varieties of wildflowers. Prodigious spring bloom is provided by bulb flowers, azaleas, rhododendrons, lilacs, quinces, dogwoods, and cornelian cherries (*Cornus mas*), while summer is vibrant with daylilies, foxgloves, hollyhocks, lavender, phlox, shasta daisies, peonies, roses, and more.

The Jeremiah Lee Mansion is the home of the Marblehead Historic Society. The estate's gardens have been planned and maintained since 1936 by the Marblehead Garden Club, which receives support from contributions and an annual plant sale held in May.

BOTANIC GARDEN OF SMITH COLLEGE
Northampton

Botany and horticulture have held positions of importance in the Smith College curriculum as far back as the institution's founding. Laid out by the ubiquitous Olmsted brothers in the late 1890s, the college's 125-acre campus was intended to function as a botanic garden and arboretum. Today, the beautifully landscaped grounds showcase more than 3,000 kinds of plants for the edification and enjoyment of students and visitors alike. Mature tree and shrub specimens, many rare and unusual, comprise the arboretum, while the botanic garden features a rock garden and an extensive herbaceous garden with a wide variety of flowering plants. The 1895 Lyman Plant House, a conservatory in the Victorian mode, shelters an outstanding collection of tropicals, including palms, orchids, ferns, and begonias. Yearly specialty displays on the grounds number a spring bulb show in March and a chrysanthemum festival in November.

The Botanic Garden of Smith College is enlivened by a show of bulbs in spring.

Roses, such as 'Chrysler Imperial', enrich the Ropes Mansion garden.

ROPES MANSION
Salem

Built in 1727 and remodeled in 1894, the historic Ropes Mansion contains magnificent collections of eighteenth- and nineteenth-century furnishings and accessories. Though designed in 1912, its little jewel of a formal garden befits the period of the house and its trappings. Outfitted with fifteen spacious beds of annuals in a formal geometric configuration, the one-acre landscape also includes a pond with water lilies and goldfish and a variety of trees and shrubs originally provided by the Arnold Arboretum (see p. 37). The site of a number of horticultural activities, with an annual lecture series held every March, the mansion and garden are maintained and operated by the Essex Institute, an organization that oversees eight historic house properties in Salem.

HERITAGE PLANTATION OF SANDWICH
Sandwich

The property, from 1921 to 1943, of Charles O. Dexter, internationally known rhododendron hybridizer, the 76-acre, beautifully landscaped Heritage Plantation features 35,000 Dexter rhododendrons in bloom in May and June and over 550 varieties of daylilies in summer. More than 1,000 kinds of trees, shrubs, and flowers overall dot the nature trails and woodlands of what today is a museum complex devoted to collections of Americana. Vintage automobiles, Currier and Ives lithographs, antique firearms, tin soldiers, dolls, and rare old tools are among the many fascinating objects on hand in a number of buildings on the property. Opened to the public in 1969, the plantation is one of New England's most popular family attractions. In addition to the permanent exhibits, concerts, family entertainment, and special events are scheduled throughout the summer.

An old windmill, among Heritage Plantation's examples of early Americana.

BERKSHIRE GARDEN CENTER
Stockbridge

The Berkshire Garden Center is a thriving community haven for horticultural enthusiasts of all kinds. Offering visual inspiration and helpful information, the 15-acre facility features colorful perennials and annuals, as well as plantings of herbs, vegetables, and dwarf conifers. A Primrose Path offers a splash of vivid color in May and June and more than 2,000 varieties of daylilies delight the eye in June and August. Tropical greenhouse collections and other informative displays provide interest throughout the year. The historic eighteenth-century Center House schedules ongoing exhibits of art, cut flower arrangements, and house plants. A rose garden, perennial borders, and wildflower trails contribute to the setting's something-for-all character, while broad lawns relieve the eye and invite the weary traveler to rest a spell.

A group of both year-round and summer Berkshire residents, who liked to garden and were looking to establish a site where they could share their

Colorful foliage brightens the Berkshire Garden Center in fall.

horticultural lore, consult professionals, and improve their knowledge of raising ornamentals and food crops in the rugged Berkshire Mountains, established the center in 1934. Today the institution has an extensive educational program that provides courses and programs for adults and children at all levels of proficiency.

The nonprofit facility is supported in large part by the dues of its members, private donations, fund-raising events, and not least of all by the tireless efforts of its ranks of dedicated volunteers. The Herb Associates, a volunteer group, prepare vinegars, dressings, sauces, jellies, moth deterrents, and other herb-derived products from plants they grow and dry themselves. These are then displayed for sale in the Herb Products Shop located on the grounds.

A graceful stairway, a Fletcher Steele design, embellishes Naumkeag.

NAUMKEAG
Stockbridge

With its gables and weathered shingles rising above sumptuous gardens, Naumkeag testifies to the comfortable largess of country living among the rich at the turn of the century. Designed by Stanford White in 1885, the 26-room mansion was the summer home of Caroline Sterling Choate and Joseph Hodges Choate (1832–1919). A prominent attorney, Mr. Choate named the 50-acre estate for his birthplace, Salem, Massachusetts, which the Native Americans called Naumkeag, meaning "place of rest."

The original landscape for the steep site in the Berkshire Hills was laid out by Nathan Barrett, who installed two broad lawn terraces and the evergreens at the north of the house. Continuing to summer at the estate after the death of her parents, Mabel Choate engaged the distinguished landscape architect Fletcher Steele to revitalize the existing plan. The completed seven-acre garden is a wonderful example of the clever uses a steeply sloping hillside can be put to, and ranks today among the designer's finest work. Immediately off the south side of the house, he created the Afternoon Garden, an "outdoor room" defined by a series of colorful Venetian-style posts connected by garlands of woodbine. These provide a degree of privacy while subtly framing views of the distant hills. Leading away from this terrace, a path with water coursing down its center directs the visitor to one of Steele's most famous designs, a series of four double staircases, each with its own fountain.

Further delights of the grounds, each gently leading into the other, are the Linden Walk, an orchard, Oriental tree peonies (in bloom in May), a Chinese pagoda, beds of floribunda roses, an allee of clipped arborvitae, a reflecting pool surrounded by late-summer displays of Spanish-bayonets

(*Yucca aloifolia*), and, through a moon gate, a Chinese garden with stone figures and ginkgo trees.

Its rooms filled with the Choate family's priceless collections of Chinese porcelain, antique furniture, rugs, and tapestries, Naumkeag is owned and maintained by The Trustees of Reservations. Dedicated to rescuing and preserving exceptional properties throughout the state since 1891, this nonprofit organization has acquired by gift or purchase 71 historic home sites, all open to the public (see Sedgwick Gardens, p. 32).

OLD STURBRIDGE VILLAGE
Sturbridge

Old Sturbridge Village offers a glimpse of what life in America was like more than 150 years ago. As a re-creation of an 1830s New England town, the 200-acre complex maintains 40 restored houses, plus gardens, shops, meeting houses, mills, and a farm. "Villagers" in dress of the period go about their domestic lives, occupations, and community activities for the historical enlightenment of visitors.

Early nineteenth-century horticultural practices are reflected in several vegetable and ornamental dooryard and cottage gardens, as well as an herb garden containing more than 300 kinds grown at the time for culinary and medicinal purposes. Practical methods of fruit and vegetable winter-keeping by drying, pickling, and root-cellar storage are also presented.

First open to the public in 1946, Old Sturbridge Village has had many decades to research and catalog the kinds and varieties of plants, sometimes better than today's, that were grown at a simpler, less chemically oriented time. This living museum has long been a conscientious disseminator of authentic, practical horticultural lore.

Old Sturbridge Village explores the gardening styles of the early 1800s.

The Vale's camellia green-house offers showy bloom in late winter.

LYMAN ESTATE, THE VALE
Waltham

One of the finest examples in the United States of a country manse in the English manner, Lyman Estate, also known as The Vale, was built in 1793 by wealthy Boston merchant, entrepreneur, and horticulturist Theodore Lyman (1753–1839). To realize his dream of a self-sustaining rural homestead, he acquired 150 acres of land, a parcel that, by the time of his death, had grown to 400 acres encompassing ornamental ponds, meadows, woodlands, a deer park, greenhouses, gardens, and a working farm.

In 1952 the Lyman family donated The Vale to The Society for the Preservation of New England Antiquities, an organization that was founded in 1910 and now owns and operates 34 house museums and properties throughout New England (see Hamilton House, p. 31, and Codman House, p. 38). Designated a National Historic Landmark, the Lyman Estate today is dominated by a remarkably preserved manor house designed by Samuel McIntire in 1793, and includes three greenhouses and 37 acres of woodlands, gardens, and cultivated fields. Largely unchanged since its inception, the landscape is one of the few surviving examples on these shores of eighteenth-century English naturalistic design.

Among the homestead's most fascinating aspects to the gardener are its greenhouses, evidence of the devotion to horticulture rampant among the gentry of Boston in the early years of the Republic. Built in 1804 to raise such tropical fruits as citrus, pineapple, and banana, The Grape House today shelters rambling Hamburg grape vines, the progeny of cuttings taken in 1870 from Hampton Court in England. The Camellia House was built around 1820 solely for the cultivation of this exotic flower, first introduced to America in 1797 via Europe from its native habitats in the Orient. On view in this collection are specimens over 100 years old. In the newest of the greenhouses, built in 1930 to provide flowers for the mansion, plants of all kinds are offered for sale year-round. In addition, special shows and sales held during February, May, September, and December feature camellias, perennials, herbs grown without pesticides, and seasonal flowering plants.

Partially funded by the Massachusetts Council on the Arts and Humanities, a state agency, The Society for the Preservation of New England Antiquities is supported by grants, income from endowment, gifts, and membership, which is open to all.

Irises contribute to the tranquillity of Stanley Park's Japanese garden.

STANLEY PARK
Westfield

As the founder of Stanley Home Products, Inc., Stanley Beveridge frequently conducted meetings with sales managers and dealers in a wooded area near his home in Westfield. Seeking to preserve the beauty and tranquillity of the natural setting, he initiated the development of a park which came to be named in his honor. Today, this 180-acre playground, boasting gardens, recreational facilities, concerts, and historical exhibits, plays host to more than 200,000 young and old visitors annually.

Among the horticultural delights to be found at the site are: a formal Rose Garden, an All-America Rose Selections test site numbering 2,500 bushes representing more than 50 varieties; a Rhododendron Garden; a Japanese Garden; Flowering Garden of the World, a circular bed representing the globe, with flowering plants forming the continents; as well as the 85-acre trail-filled Memorial Wildlife Sanctuary and a five-acre Arboretum. A 100-foot-high Carillon Tower, dedicated in 1950, chimes concerts throughout the summer with its 86 English and Flemish bells. Of special appeal to children are the playground and game areas, the Covered Bridge, the Old Mill Wheel, the Blacksmith Shop displaying operational forge, bellows, anvil, and other tools, and the authentic Dinosaur Tracks.

In 1949 Stanley Park of Westfield, Inc., was established as a charitable corporation to maintain the park and ensure its permanent availability to the public.

THE CASE ESTATES
Weston

The Case Estates, a facility of the Arnold Arboretum of Harvard University (see p. 37), maintains nurseries, specialized collections, experimental and display plantings, and demonstration gardens. With temperatures in Weston averaging 13 degrees colder than at the Arnold in Jamaica Plain, nursery stock is tested here for hardiness before being installed at the Arboretum. Outstanding collections of rhododendrons (developed in conjunction with the Massachusetts Chapter of the American Rhododendron Society), daylilies, groundcovers, hostas (in association with the New England Hosta Society), and perennials, plus food-crop gardens and woodland paths, make the 112-acre site a constant source of gardening inspiration and education.

Originally belonging to Marion and Louisa Case and known as Hillcrest Gardens, the property, from 1909 to 1942, was utilized as a vegetable and fruit farm, a school for young horticulture students, and a plant introduction and display facility. Following this period, the Cases bequeathed the site to the Arnold. The years of development since then have yielded a profusion of plants that provide continuing bloom from spring to fall according to the following schedule: cornelian cherries, early azaleas, magnolias, forsythias, daffodils, and marsh-marigolds in April; crab apples, lady's slippers, azaleas, dogwoods, spireas, and redbuds in May; kousa

Vivid-hued peonies are among The Case Estates' flowering collections.

dogwoods, rhododendrons, mountain laurels, iris, daylilies, and peonies in June; ornamental onions, daylilies, hostas, clematis, stewartias, sourwoods, Turk's-cap lilies, and perennials in July; more perennials in August; and franklinias and asters in September. A rare-plant sale is held annually on the third Sunday in September.

Though administered by Harvard University, both the Arnold Arboretum and the Case Estates are financed through their own resources. All costs of operation are met through gifts, past and present, and membership, open to all to either institution.

NEW HAMPSHIRE

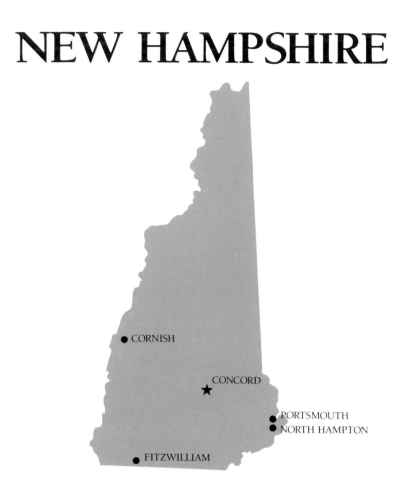

CORNISH

CONCORD

PORTSMOUTH
NORTH HAMPTON

FITZWILLIAM

SAINT-GAUDENS NATIONAL HISTORIC SITE
Cornish

This 150-acre preserve of hills, streams, ponds, and gardens was the residence of Augustus Saint-Gaudens (1848–1907), one of America's greatest sculptors, from 1885 until his death. Its complex of white structures, including the main house (*Aspet*, named after his father's birthplace in France), stables, studios, and Greek-temple–design burial memorial still echoes with the ghostly sounds of outdoor revelries, masques, and games of lawn bowling and ice hockey staged by the classically inspired, visionary artist and his high-spirited friends.

Taking great delight in gardening, the sculptor lavished attention on the grounds, transforming unkempt pastures and woodland into expanses of lawn, formal gardens, vine bowers, pools, fountains, nature trails, stands of birch, and hedges of pine and hemlock. These are maintained today by the National Park Service of the U.S. Department of the Interior, in cooperation with the trustees of the Saint-Gaudens Memorial, for the enrichment of the public. Of special note is the great variety of ferns to be found in the native woodlands. These include ostrich, maidenhair, interrupted, sensitive, and horsetail.

Legend has it that when Saint-Gaudens first saw the hilltop property and its dilapidated mansion, built in 1800 and once home to a tavern, he was reluctant to take it over. But he was about to begin work on a statue of Lincoln for a park in Chicago, and a friend who owned a house nearby helped the artist decide by telling him he would find many "Lincoln-shaped" men among the lean local Yankees.

After Saint-Gaudens' death, his widow and son provided for the preservation of the estate by deeding it to a board of trustees. Later, the New Hampshire legislature chartered the Saint-Gaudens Memorial as a non-profit corporation for the maintenance and exhibition of the house, studios, and collections. The grounds and seven furnished structures opened to the public in 1926. In 1964 Congressional legislation authorized the National Park Service to accept the property as a gift, and a year later the memorial was designated a National Historic Site.

The gardens of Saint-Gaudens are the legacy of a great American sculptor.

RHODODENDRON STATE PARK
Fitzwilliam

Crucial to the history of this beautiful preserve is the 16-acre stand of native *Rhododendron maximum* that was designated a National Natural Landmark by the National Park Service in 1982. Also listed on the National Register of Historic Places is the 1790 cottage built at the site by

Rhododendron State Park preserves a naturally occurring native example.

Capt. Samuel Patch. A subsequent owner in 1901, Levi Fuller, planned to harvest the site's lumber, but responding to the threat to the rhododendrons, Mary Lee Ware of Boston purchased the land and gave it to the Appalachian Mountain Club in 1903 with the proviso that the rhododendron grove and pine forest ". . . be held as a reservation properly protected and open to the public . . . forever." Since 1946 the site has been operated by the New Hampshire Division of Parks and Recreation. In 1977 the grove lay crushed under a tangle of fallen branches as the result of a winter storm, but the damage was eventually repaired with the help of the Fitzwilliam Garden Club.

Rhododendrons are members of the heath family, with relatives numbering blueberries, cranberries, mountain laurel, heathers, trailing arbutus, and wintergreen. This natural stand in Fitzwilliam, in bloom in mid-July, and another in Maine represent the northern limit of maximum's growing range. The naturally occurring species is most at home in the North Carolina mountains. Other features of the state park to be enjoyed as well as the rhododendrons are natural woodlands and a wildflower trail established by the Fitzwilliam Garden Club and offering something in bloom all through the spring, summer, and fall.

FULLER GARDENS
North Hampton

Once part of the summer residence of the late Alvan T. Fuller, former Governor of Massachusetts, these gardens were designed by Arthur Shurtleff in Colonial-Revival style in the early 1920s. Within view of the spectacular New Hampshire coastline, the extensive plantings take full advantage of the tempering effects of the ocean in this otherwise harsh northern location. Though the governor's house, Runnymede-by-the-Sea, no longer stands, the gardens he initiated and enjoyed over many years have been meticulously preserved and maintained by the Fuller Foundation of New Hampshire.

Tulips, rhododendrons, azaleas, wildflowers, and wisteria fill the two-acre property with color in spring, yielding to annuals and perennials in summer and chrysanthemums in fall. The 1,500-bush rose beds, an official All-America Rose Display Garden for New Hampshire, provide continuous bloom from mid-June through October. Other features include a Japanese garden and a conservatory with an extensive collection of exotic tropical and desert plants.

Mauve pulmonaria and white epimedium in Fuller Gardens in spring.

MOFFATT-LADD HOUSE AND GARDEN
Portsmouth

The innocent serenity of the late 1700s permeates the atmosphere surrounding this historic house and remarkably preserved gardens. Built by John Moffatt as a wedding gift to his son, Samuel, the house was occupied by their descendants until 1900. It was entrusted in 1912 to the National Society of the Colonial Dames of America in the State of New Hampshire.

Overlooking the Piscataqua River, the homestead is a treasure of eighteenth-century art, architecture, furnishings, and interior detailing, including a great hall with grand stairway, hand-carved paneling and moldings, and a secret tunnel that originally led down to the Moffatt Wharf and the ships that awaited there. The gardens, mostly to the back and sides of the house, were laid out in their present form by Alexander Hamilton Ladd in the mid-nineteenth century.

The grounds' formal planting beds are arranged on either side of a 300-foot axis that leads from the back of the house to a wrought-iron gate at the property's rear boundary. Of special note are a wonderful series of grass steps that lead upward to terraced flower beds. Two plantings that survive from the eighteenth century are an English damask rose planted by Mrs. Samuel Moffatt in 1768 and a giant horse chestnut tree planted by Gen. William Whipple in 1776 in celebration of his return from Philadelphia, where he had just signed the Declaration of Independence. Other plantings include a wide selection of annuals, perennials, herbs, bulbs, fruit trees, and flowering shrubs and vines. Old brick walks and a spiral trellis add to the Colonial ambience.

Beds of the Moffatt-Ladd garden, featuring the spiky flowers of gas plant.

STRAWBERY BANKE
Portsmouth

Four centuries of American history and culture come alive at this museum enclave of 35 restored buildings. So named because the English who settled the area in 1630 found an abundance of wild berries growing along the shores of the Piscataqua River, ten-acre Strawbery Banke enjoyed 150 years as a thriving waterfront community. Its prominence and prosperity waning by the nineteenth and early twentieth centuries, it evolved into an immigrant settlement known as Puddle Dock. Thanks to the efforts in the 1950s that rescued the area from demolition and urban renewal, the site today offers much to see and explore, including: seven furnished houses of varying time periods; exhibits addressing social history, architecture, and traditional trades; on-site archaeological excavations; working craft shops; historic gardens and landscapes; and a wealth of educational tours and programs for the whole family.

The garden restorations at the museum facility are as carefully and authentically conceived as the buildings they adorn. These include: the Sherburne House Garden (ca. 1720), based on deed research and archaeological findings, with raised beds of vegetables and herbs and an orchard of period-variety apple trees; the Goodwin Mansion Garden (ca. 1850–1890), an elaborate Victorian garden re-created from the diary of Sarah Goodwin and an 1862 landscape plan, with lavish displays of spring bulbs, summer annuals and perennials, and flowering shrubs; and the Thomas Bailey Aldrich Garden (ca. 1907), a splendid example of Colonial-Revival design, with urn-topped posts, arbors, and such evocative flowers as heliotrope, pinks, lilies, roses, phlox, and mignonette. In addition to the historic installations, modern-day display gardens at Strawbery Banke include a 160-foot-long perennial walkway, an herb garden, and a cutting garden containing Betty Prior roses, callery pears, climbing hydrangeas, rock cotoneaster, and annuals in raised beds.

Accredited by the American Association of Museums and listed in the National Register of Historic Places, the restored village offers a wide variety of special events and programs for children and adults, ranging from New England Gardening Day in June to a Fall Festival in October and a Candlelight Stroll in December. Strawbery Banke is a nonprofit organization supported in part by contributions and membership.

Strawbery Banke's Sherburne Garden, tended by a costumed "villager."

NEW JERSEY

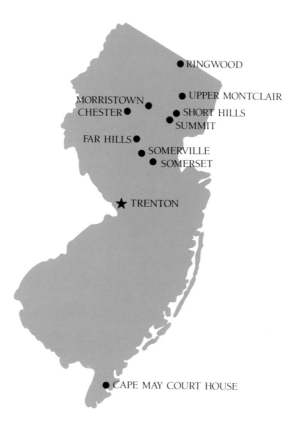

RINGWOOD

MORRISTOWN
CHESTER

UPPER MONTCLAIR
SHORT HILLS
SUMMIT

FAR HILLS

SOMERVILLE
SOMERSET

★ TRENTON

CAPE MAY COURT HOUSE

LEAMING'S RUN GARDENS AND COLONIAL FARM
Cape May Court House

Leaming's Run has been called one of the most beautiful gardens in the United States. As a showplace of annuals, the installation rightfully deserves the accolade. On 30 acres of coastal forest in the southernmost end of New Jersey, Jack Aprill, owner, designer, and planter of the landscape, has created not one garden, but 27, each to be discovered in a natural clearing as one wanders along a sandy path past ponds, bogs, streams, and hummingbirds. While color schemes dictate the annual flowers of some of the gardens—the yellow, pink, blue and white, orange, red and blue, and white and red gardens, for example—others are devoted to one particular kind of annual, such as snapdragons, begonias, or celosias. Still others in the endlessly imaginative succession of plantings include English-cottage, shade, fern, rose, houseplant, and everlasting gardens.

The Colonial Farm, tucked into the deepest reaches of the woodland, features a one-room log cabin built by Aprill according to records left by whaler Christopher Leaming, the property's first settler. These indicated that Leaming and his family lived in such a structure in the late 1600s until a more permanent residence could be built. The tobacco, cotton, wheat, sugar cane, and herbs that grow in the cabin clearing, as well as the farm animals in the vicinity, are authentic to the period.

Having constructed the gardens almost single-handedly over a period of five years, Aprill opened his labor of love to the public in 1977. His aim was to reveal to the average gardener the wealth of interest that could be derived from the simplest, most readily available ornamentals. The best time to enjoy peak bloom is late May through early October.

A garden devoted solely to begonias may be found at Leaming's Run.

Underplantings of lamb's ears complement clipped yews at Willowwood.

WILLOWWOOD ARBORETUM
Chester

This splendid 130-acre preserve of gardens, meadows, and forests in the Hacklebarney Hills is a former private estate dating from 1792. Thanks to the Tubb brothers, who purchased the property in 1908 and immediately began a private collection of rare species, the gardens today offer more than 3,500 kinds of plants. These include an enormous variety of oaks, 110 kinds of willows, and 50 different maples, along with conifers, hollies, wildflowers, a hillside carpeted with pink lady's slippers, a 70-foot dawn redwood, and major collections of magnolias, cherries, and lilacs. All of these delights, including a children's garden, are made accessible by pleasant, informal paths that wander throughout the grounds. An active education program is directed at all age groups. Like the Frelinghuysen Arboretum (see p. 57), Willowwood is overseen by the preservation-minded Morris County Park Commission.

LEONARD J. BUCK GARDEN
Far Hills

When the Wisconsin ice sheet began its retreat from the Far Hills, New Jersey, area some 12,000 years ago, it left a pond and stream hollow punctuated with dramatic rock outcroppings. The site would have been daunting to most gardeners, but Leonard J. Buck, its owner, recognized its potential as a naturalized landscape. In the late 1930s, with the assistance of Zenon Schreiber, a rock garden designer, he set about planting alpines, heathers, and ferns, with the aim of creating an ecologically sound environment that was not recognizably touched by human hands. The intervening years of growth have lent the Leonard J. Buck Garden the maturity it needed to fulfill its mandate, and today the 33-acre site is a fascinating series of woodland vignettes, each with its own slightly varying microclimate and associative plants.

A wild sunflower (Helianthus) *at the Leonard J. Buck Garden.*

One of the greatest pleasures in experiencing this garden is discovering the enormous variety of plants that are tucked among its rockeries and along its trails. Native wildflowers are insistent throughout, and the extraordinary F. Gordon Foster Hardy Fern Collection, brought from Sparta, New Jersey, to the site in the fall of 1986, fills a slope with Christmas, ostrich, northern maidenhair, interrupted, cinnamon, painted, and autumn kinds, among others. An abundance of heaths and heathers, comprising varieties of erica, calluna, and bruckenthalia, forms a rare gathering of these delightfully colorful, ground-covering shrubs, many of which bloom into late fall and winter. A host of exotic alpine plants, azaleas, and rhododendrons competes for attention in the spring. The installation was donated by Helen Buck to the Somerset County Park Commission in 1976.

Frelinghuysen's manor house, part of an estate once called Whippany Farm.

FRELINGHUYSEN ARBORETUM
Morristown

A stately Colonial-Revival mansion built in 1891 and surrounded by 127 acres of gardens, fields, and woodlands is preserved today as the George Griswold Frelinghuysen Arboretum. Morristown was a fashionable summer address for prominent families of the late nineteenth century. When George Frelinghuysen, an attorney and the son of Frederick T. Frelinghuysen, Secretary of State under Chester A. Arthur, married Sarah Ballantine, he chose the area to build a commodious summer estate, which he and his wife dubbed Whippany Farm. Inheriting the property from her parents, Mathilda E. Frelinghuysen participated in the plans to convert the private estate into a public arboretum, and ultimately bequeathed it in 1969 to the people of Morris County, ensuring that the unique warmth and charm of Whippany Farm would be preserved for all.

More than four miles of trails investigate the sprawling, majestic property, encountering a formal rose garden, a lilac garden, an azalea trail, flowering dogwood, apple, magnolia, and cherry trees, berried hollies, rhododendrons, viburnums, spring bulbs, peonies, carpets of wildflowers, home demonstration gardens, and a braille walk. The plantings are thoughtfully designed to display continuous color from early spring into fall. Headquarters of the Morris County Park Commission, overseers of this and 23 other settings throughout the county, the site is a regional center of horticultural activities of all kinds, including various educational programs at its Joseph F. Haggarty, Jr., Education Center. The Friends of the Frelinghuysen Arboretum support the arboretum's endeavors and offer membership to all.

SKYLANDS
Ringwood

Skylands at Ringwood State Park in the Ramapo Mountains is an estate in the grand manner, a 45-room Tudor-Revival, granite mansion, designed by John Russell Pope, surrounded by 96 acres of formal gardens and over 1,000 acres of meadows and woodlands. The site was first occupied by Francis Lynde Stetson (1846–1920), a prominent New York lawyer and a trustee of the New York Botanical Garden (see p. 75). Stetson chose Samuel Parsons, Jr., a protégé of Frederick Law Olmsted, to lay out Skylands' grounds, roads, ponds, and drainage systems.

Another trustee of NYBG, investment banker Clarence McKenzie Lewis (1877–1959), purchased the estate in 1922 and engaged the distinguished

A Skylands annual bed combines blue and scarlet sages with dusty miller.

firm of Vitale and Geiffert to expand the gardens. Major features of their work remaining today are the West Terrace and the Terrace Gardens. Lewis was an inveterate plant collector who imported specimens from such remote places as Afghanistan, the Belgian Congo, New Zealand, and Kashmir. No matter how unlikely the possibility, he would try to grow a rare plant at his estate if he thought it had the slightest chance of survival.

In 1953 the estate was sold to Shelton College, which occupied it as a campus until 1966 when it was purchased by the State of New Jersey. The state undertook a major capital improvement program, building a new greenhouse and restoring the grounds. Today, these contain approximately 5,000 species and varieties of plants, some unique to Skylands: a climbing hydrangea (*Hydrangea petiolaris*, 'Skylands Giant'), at the entrance to the manor house; a golden form of Oriental spruce (*Picea orientalis*) called "Skylands"; and a dwarf, dark-purple iris (*Iris cristata*), "Skylands Iris."

The formal gardens immediately surrounding the mansion include the Perennial Border and Annual, Winter, Azalea, Octagonal, Summer, and Peony Gardens. Crab Apple Vista, filling a half-mile slope with bloom, Magnolia Walk, the Lilac Collection (over 400 varieties), and thousands of bulbs greet the spring with color. Naturalized areas include the Rhododendron, Heather, Bog, and Wildflower Gardens, Barberry and Horse-Chestnut Collections, the Dry and Swan-Pond Meadows, and miles of woodland paths.

Skylands Association was founded in 1976 as a membership support group to help maintain and preserve the site, develop educational programs, and secure volunteers. In 1984 Gov. Thomas Kean officially designated the Skylands gardens as the New Jersey State Botanical Garden.

CORA HARTSHORN ARBORETUM AND BIRD SANCTUARY
Short Hills

For untamed woodland beauty, wildflowers, and the sport of bird watching, the Cora Hartshorn Arboretum is the place to visit. On 16½ acres of rises and gullies along a glacial moraine in a residential area of Short Hills, the sanctuary is a microcosm of the area's natural beauty. Three miles of trails are ablaze with foliage color in fall and abloom in spring with laurel, azaleas, rhododendrons, and more than 80 varieties of wildflowers, ranging from Christmas rose in March to lady's slippers in May.

The preserve was begun by Cora Hartshorn in 1923 on land given to her by her father, Stewart Hartshorn, the founder of Short Hills. When "Miss Cora" died in 1958, the arboretum was bequeathed to Millburn Township. In 1961 an Arboretum Association was created. Its Board of Directors oversees planning, development, and programming, and the township maintains the trails, grounds, and buildings. A distinguished lodgelike edifice called Stone House greets visitors at the grounds' entrance. Handsomely fashioned of fieldstone and traprock, it was designed by Bernhardt E. Muller, a master of stone construction. Serving as the arboretum's center of activities, it shelters nature exhibits, educational programs, and a small coterie of live woodland animals.

Fall finds Hartshorn Arboretum's Stone House enveloped in foliage color.

RUDOLF W. VAN DER GOOT ROSE GARDEN OF COLONIAL PARK
Somerset

This magnificent collection of 4,000 rosebushes representing 275 varieties is both the creation of and a tribute to Rudolf W. van der Goot, Somerset County Park Commission's first horticulturist. Established over a seven-year period beginning in 1971, the one-acre installation, made up of three connecting sections, each with its own distinct geometric plan, is a lesson in classic formal rose garden design.

Capped by a graceful gazebo, the first area, the Mettler Garden, is a holdover from a working farm, known as the Mettler Estate, that originally occupied the site. Rectangular in design, it features a central fountain surrounded by a planting of miniature roses and beds of modern hybrid teas. The Center Garden, circular in plan, is bisected by a straight walkway containing beds of polyantha roses. Completing the broad half circles that flank the walkway are beds of hybrid teas, grandifloras, and floribundas, and lining the perimeter of the garden are redwood trellises supporting a variety of climbing roses. As its name suggests, the Dutch Garden, square in plan and the last of the sections, is designed in the traditional style of a formal rose garden in Holland. Its beds, edged with candytuft, are planted with heritage roses, species and hybrids that evolved long before the mid-1800s when hybrid teas began to be introduced.

The van der Goot Garden has been an official All-America Rose Selections test facility since 1973. Administered by the Somerset County Park

Commission, Colonial Park is also the site of two other facilities definitely worth visiting: a Fragrance and Sensory Garden, with raised beds planted with 80 species of fragrant and interestingly textured plants labeled in braille, and a 144-acre arboretum displaying evergreens, dwarf conifers, and flowering trees and shrubs, including 200 lilac bushes.

The van der Goot Rose Garden, with the Mettler Garden in the foreground.

DUKE GARDENS
Somerville

A series of 11 greenhouse rooms, each connected to the other, Duke Gardens is an astounding and unique experience, like no other you are likely to encounter. Each of the rooms encases a meticulous full-scale re-creation, down to the last detail, of a particular kind of garden from a certain era or world locale. The settings represent Chinese, Japanese, English, French, Italian, Indo-Persian, Colonial, Edwardian, American Desert, and Tropical Jungle inspiration. Strolling from one to the other is like a storybook tour of history's fabled gardens, and a visit during the winter when the ground outdoors is blanketed with snow makes the creations seem that much more miraculous.

The French Garden, my particular favorite, trimmed with endless variations on the theme of elaborate treillage (latticework), transports one to eighteenth-century France and the gardens of the great châteaus. A landscape in the English manner features the requisite sumptuous perennial borders, and a rose-bedecked Islamic garden is bisected by a channel of water in the Persian tradition. Enclosed in what were originally utilitarian greenhouses built by James Duke for his New Jersey estate, the gardens represent the singular vision, horticultural knowledge, and unrivaled sense of aesthetics of his daughter, Doris Duke, who oversaw their creation and made them accessible to the public. She donated 11 acres of her estate, encompassing the gardens, to the Duke Gardens Foundation, Inc., and the facility was opened to the public in 1964.

Sprightly tulips contribute to the floriferous English garden at Duke.

REEVES-REED ARBORETUM
Summit

A handsome Colonial-Revival residence arose on the site of Reeves-Reed Arboretum in 1889. Today it houses the administrative and educational center for this conscientiously information-oriented institution. Back in the latter part of the nineteenth century, the owner of the estate, John Horner Wisner, hired New York landscape architect Calvert Vaux, a partner of Frederick Law Olmsted, to plan the grounds. Although Vaux's plans were never executed, Mrs. Wisner planted daffodils in a large glacial hollow, and each April, a much-enlarged daffodil display is a major Reeves-Reed attraction. New owners of the property in 1916, Mr. and Mrs. Richard Reeves, expanded the daffodil plantings and started rose and rock gardens in 1925. The estate's last private owners, the Charles L. Reed family, added a circular herb garden and created a woodland trail in the 1960s. The property was elevated to the distinction of an arboretum when local citizens raised half its purchase price to save its natural beauty from oblivion. The city of Summit matched these funds, and in 1974 the 12½ acres of formal gardens, rolling lawns, open fields, wetlands and woodlands became a permanent preserve.

In spring, the arboretum is a showplace of azaleas, rhododendrons, wildflowers, flowering trees, and daffodils by the thousands. The Susan Graham Reeves Rose Garden blooms from June to September and field flowers, lilies, and ever-changing serpentine perennial beds from April to October. As a center of horticultural and environmental education, the institution offers children a hands-on Discovery Center and a nature study program in cooperation with area schools. Lectures, classes, field trips, and concerts round out the offerings for adults. Reeves-Reed is a nonprofit corporation supported by contributions and membership dues.

A bounteous summer perennial border at Reeves-Reed Arboretum.

Presby Gardens are a celebration of the perfection of the iris.

PRESBY MEMORIAL IRIS GARDENS
Upper Montclair

Established in 1927 in honor of Frank H. Presby, founder of the American Iris Society, the Presby Memorial Iris Gardens promise a spectacular display of color and waves of heady fragrance from the third week of May to the second week of June. Planted with more than 6,000 iris varieties from all over the world, many dating as far back as the 1500s, this National Historic Landmark located along a brook in Mountainside Park is a joint venture of the Township of Montclair, the Montclair Garden Club, and the Citizen's Committee of the Garden.

The oldest known irises of history progress to the newest introductions as one walks from north to south along the rectangular beds. In addition to the May–June period mentioned above—peak bloom time for tall, bearded varieties—dwarf and median irises bloom around May 10, Siberian, Louisiana, Spuria, and Japanese, from late May into July, and a group of remontants (repeat bloomers), in late September and October.

NEW YORK

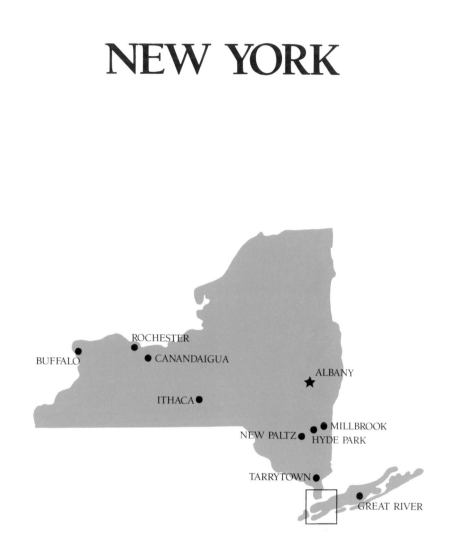

BUFFALO
ROCHESTER
CANANDAIGUA
ITHACA
ALBANY
NEW PALTZ
MILLBROOK
HYDE PARK
TARRYTOWN
GREAT RIVER

CLARK GARDEN
Albertson

Once the home of Grenville and Fanny Dwight Clark, this 12-acre property was donated by Mr. Clark to the Brooklyn Botanic Garden (see p. 77)
in 1966, upon the death of his wife. Since that time it has developed into
an attractive and authoritative source of ideas readily adaptable by the
suburban homeowner. A mix of woodlands, ponds, and rockeries, the
landscape is an ideal setting for 15 thematically defined display areas:
roses, irises, rhododendrons, azaleas, wildflowers, daylilies, dwarf conifers, herbs, low-maintenance perennials, unusual annuals, spring bulbs,
groundcovers, plus shade, apiary, and rock gardens. The garden showcases
a variety of unusual trees and shrubs that flower out of season, and its

children's and seniors' vegetable gardens offer ideas tailored to the needs of these special groups.

Clark Garden became independent of the Brooklyn Botanic Garden in January 1990. It is now operated under the ownership of the town of North Hempstead, which is committed to maintaining the facility's public botanic-garden status permanently.

Clark Garden's rock garden combines alpines with dwarf conifers.

BUFFALO AND ERIE COUNTY BOTANICAL GARDENS
Buffalo

The centerpiece of the Buffalo and Erie County Botanical Gardens is a graceful Victorian-style conservatory designed and built by the greenhouse manufacturer Lord and Burnham in the late 1890s. Its surrounding 11 acres are situated in Buffalo's South Park, one of six in the system of green oases laid out for the city by no less than Frederick Law Olmsted.

The conservatory's 67-foot-high central dome caps palms from the Americas, Pacific Islands, and the Mediterranean. A catwalk negotiates a waterfall in the ferns, hydrophytes, and cycads section, and children learn how plants are used for food, clothing, and medicine in the hands-on section, the Marketplace. Others among the marvels to be found within the glass wings and domes of this rambling structure are the bromeliad and hanging plant, edible fruit, orchid and anthuria, and cacti collections. The Show House offers spring, autumn, and Christmas floral displays, and Assorted Plants exhibits a selection that can be grown in anyone's outdoor garden.

In 1981 when Erie County assumed ownership of the South Park Botanical Gardens from the City of Buffalo, the aging facility was in need of repair. Recognizing its historical and architectural significance, the county renamed it and embarked on a major program of renovation. Aided by state, federal, and private grants, efforts are ongoing to restore the gardens to their turn-of-the-century glory. The conservatory was added to the National Register of Historic Places in 1982.

Bromeliads bloom in Buffalo and Erie's vintage conservatory.

SONNENBERG GARDENS
Canandaigua

Sonnenberg (German for "Sunny Hill") is one of the great turn-of-the-century estates, with every accoutrement attended to and with endless delights to be discovered on its grounds' 50 acres. It was purchased in 1863 by Frederick Ferris Thompson, a co-founder of the First National City Bank of New York, and his wife, Mary Clark Thompson. After razing the original house, the couple built an imposing 40-room, turreted stone mansion with a sweeping veranda. One among many of their residences in various locations, Sonnenberg became the place the Thompsons enjoyed spending summers and Christmases.

A pond at Sonnenberg, part of Ernest Bowditch's plan for the great estate.

The estate's great gardens first saw the light of day between 1902 and 1916, when Mrs. Thompson commissioned Ernest W. Bowditch of Boston to design an overall landscape in memory of her husband, who died in 1899. Renowned as the landscape architect of The Breakers (see p. 101) for Cornelius Vanderbilt Whitney and of Cleveland's public park system, Bowditch conceived a plan that included lawns, ponds, a conservatory, the Italian Garden, its belvedere (a garden structure whose name is Italian for "beautiful view"), and probably the Rose Garden. The subsequent Blue and White Garden, Moonlight Garden, Rock Garden, Pansy Garden, and Sub Rosa Garden were designed by Bowditch's associate, John Handrahan, with Mrs. Thompson exercising considerable influence. Under her guidance, K. Wadamori designed Sonnenberg's Japanese Garden, with its traditional teahouse.

Completed in 1916, the gardens, along with a deer park and a number of aviaries, were generously opened by Mrs. Thompson to thousands of people on various days throughout the year. After her death in 1923, the estate passed to a nephew, who sold it to the United States government in 1931. In 1972 the President of the United States signed a law establishing a nonprofit corporation to restore and exhibit the mansion and gardens for public study and enjoyment. Following the restoration efforts of over 200 volunteers from the Canandaigua community, the grounds were opened to the public in 1973.

Collectively recognized by the Smithsonian Institution as "one of the most magnificent late Victorian gardens ever created in America," the installations mentioned above have all been lovingly re-created. The visitor truly feels to-the-manor-born when wandering among: the Italian Garden, with its fleur-de-lis-design parterres realized with coleus, dusty miller, and sweet alyssum in summer; the Conservatory, built in 1903 by Lord and Burnham, containing a collection of tropicals and desert plants; the Moonlight Garden, planted only with white flowers (nicotiana, tuberose, arabis, yucca, and cimicifuga); and the Rose Garden, with over 4,000 bushes of red, pink, and white roses. Also fascinating are the many specimen trees planted by the Thompsons' distinguished guests. Outstanding ornamental elements to be found on the grounds include the Roman Bath, Temple of Diana, and the classic pergola separating the Italian and Rose gardens.

Memberships and generous financial contributions support the continuing restorations and cultural events at Sonnenberg.

BAYARD CUTTING ARBORETUM
Great River

Originally the manor of William Bayard Cutting, this parklike preserve features the most extensive collection of firs, spruces, pines, cypress, hemlocks, yews, and lesser-known conifers to be found on Long Island. Once heavily wooded, the grounds were cleared and replanted in 1887 according to plans drawn up by Frederick Law Olmsted's landscape architecture firm. Many of the old specimen oaks found on the property today date from the original forests.

The Tudor-style mansion that dominates the preserve contains magnificent fireplaces, woodworkings, stained-glass windows, and a small natural history museum featuring a remarkable collection of mounted birds. The extensive plantings surrounding the structure include rhododendrons, azaleas, hollies, and dwarf evergreens, and several native woodland locations on the property yield bursts of wildflowers and daffodils. The ponds and streamlets scattered throughout encourage gatherings of aquatic birds and small-mammal wildlife.

The estate was donated to the Long Island State Park Region by Mrs. Cutting and her daughter, Mrs. Olivia James, "to provide an oasis of beauty and quiet for the pleasure, rest and refreshment of those who delight in outdoor beauty; and to bring about a greater appreciation and understanding of the value and importance of informal planting."

Native woodlands frame a bridge-traversed pond at Bayard Cutting.

Vanderbilt Mansion's ornate beds, evidence of methodical restoration.

VANDERBILT MANSION NATIONAL HISTORIC SITE
Hyde Park

Probably the most elaborate of the great houses built by the Hudson River Valley land barons of the late 1800s and early 1900s, the 50-room limestone Vanderbilt Mansion, designed by McKim, Mead and White in Beaux-Arts style, was the pride of Frederick W. Vanderbilt who purchased the site in 1895. Its already existing Italian-style formal gardens had been laid out in the early 1800s by Belgian landscape architect André Parmentier for the estate's previous owner, Dr. David Hosack. Having found the ideal canvas for expressing his devotion to horticulture, Vanderbilt, who held a degree in the subject from Yale, added terraced gardens, a cherry allee, a rose garden, pools, statuary, and propagation greenhouses.

The Federal Government was bequeathed the property in 1940, after Vanderbilt's death, and with funding for the maintenance of the gardens scarce during the war, weeds and brush took over and the walls and statuary began to crumble. The National Park Service initiated restoration efforts in 1974 and by 1987 the walls and structures, the upper and lower annual beds, and the cherry tree walk had been rebuilt and replanted. Also restored during this period were the pool garden and the rose garden, installed with over 4,000 perennials and more than 1,000 bushes, respectively.

As magnificent as they are today, the Vanderbilt gardens are still in the process of rediscovery. The noble effort to resurrect them entirely is funded by contributions and sustained by Volunteers in Park, a dedicated group of people who cultivate and maintain the existing gardens and act as guides, interpreting the ongoing stages of restoration for visitors.

CORNELL PLANTATIONS
Ithaca

Encompassing 2,900 acres adjacent to the beautiful Cornell campus, this horticultural wonderland includes a botanic garden, an arboretum, and natural areas abounding with lakes, streams, gorges, and waterfalls. Well-planned trails course through forests and along deeply cut and craggy Fall Creek and Cascadilla gorges, affording spectacular views of Lake Cayuga and the surrounding countryside. The 1,500-acre arboretum offers a rich diversity of trees and flowering shrubs in landscaped settings.

Also a source of education and inspiration for students and visitors alike is the botanic garden, with such excellently conceived installations as: the Walter C. Heasley, Jr., Rock Garden; the Mundy Wildflower Garden; the formal Robison York State Herb Garden; the Heritage Crops Collection; the Clement Gray Bowers Rhododendron Collection; the Mary Rockwell Azalea Garden; the International Crop and Weed Garden; the W. C.

A sweeping, tree-studded landscape at Cornell Plantations' arboretum.

Muenscher Poisonous Plants Garden; alpine plants; flowering crab apples; the American Peony Society Garden, with a selection of annuals and perennials; and the Pinetum. Established in 1935, the Liberty Hyde Bailey Hortorium, named for the celebrated horticulturist and located on the Cornell campus, is a greenhouse containing a diverse collection of tropical and desert plants.

The Cornell University Arboretum was the vision of Nelson Wells, a protégé of Olmsted's, who completed the facility's plans in 1938. The plantation's name and much of its early development are attributed to Liberty Hyde Bailey.

BAILEY ARBORETUM
Lattingtown

Featuring a house built in 1800 and 42 tranquil acres, this sprawling estate was once the summer home of Mr. and Mrs. Frank Bailey. Having collected trees from all over the world, including many rare species, for his country property, Mr. Bailey bequeathed the site to Nassau County in 1968. Memorable features of the grounds today include a rose garden, a perennial border, an iris garden, a rock garden, and a vast collection of more than

Voluptuous hybrids work their magic in Bailey Arboretum's rose garden.

600 kinds of trees and shrubs. Tulips, daffodils, and chrysanthemums add seasonal color, and the entire facility is maintained by the Nassau County Department of Recreation and Parks.

THE JOHN P. HUMES JAPANESE STROLL GARDEN
Mill Neck

The experience the John P. Humes Japanese Stroll Garden evokes is that of a walking meditation. In the Japanese landscape tradition of an idealized, "naturalized" setting revealed in stages, sometimes fooling the eye and manipulating the observer, the sylvan setting prods one to shed worldly attachments and form a timeless bond with nature.

During a visit to Japan in 1960, Ambassador and Mrs. John P. Humes became irrevocably enchanted with its landscaping. They brought back a teahouse, which now adorns this garden, and a Japanese gardener and his wife. Over a period of four years, they transformed four acres of sloping, forested land on Long Island's North Shore, working within the dictates of the existing topography, into the Stroll Garden as it is today.

Wandering along the garden's paths, one is aware of the Japanese principles of "hide and reveal" and "movement along the diagonal," as opposed to the straight line. Paths twist to and fro, serving to divert views, reveal vistas sequentially, and enlarge spatial relationships. Another consideration is the balance of opposites, "yin" against "yang." Plants, the yin, or flesh, of the garden must be balanced with stone and other elements, the yang, or the garden's bones. Finally, water is essential as the setting's lifeblood.

The cherry trees, maples, hollies, azaleas, lady's slippers, ferns, pines, and irises that abound promote the contemplative Asian mood, abetted by such nonplant elements as lanterns, stepping stones, waterfalls, bridges, and gates.

Ambassador Humes gave the garden to the North Shore Wildlife Sanctuary in 1980. The Humes Foundation, Inc., continues to provide personnel and maintenance funding.

Lady's slippers foster the Asian atmosphere of the Humes Stroll Garden.

INNISFREE GARDEN
Millbrook

Innisfree is a unique experience. The creation, some 60 years ago, of artist Walter Beck and his wife Marion Burt Stone, a botanist, the "garden" appears, at first sight, to be a naturalized woodland cradled within a lake-bottomed valley. But closer inspection reveals the artful and sensitive manipulation of nature that is the hallmark of this contemplative, spiritually imbued setting.

Inspired by ancient Chinese scrolls found on a trip to London, Mr. and Mrs. Beck returned to their 1,000-acre land holding in Millbrook with the idea of applying the age-old concept of the Chinese "cup" garden to a particular glen on a portion of their acreage. They reshaped the terrain, moving glacial rocks to redirect streams or create enclosures, always taking care not to disturb fragile accumulations of mosses and lichens. They selected smaller stones to become pieces of sculpture, standing them alone on end or joining them with others in bold arrangements.

Innisfree unfolds to the visitor as a series of scenic experiences, smaller cups within the large one of the valley. In the Chinese tradition, each cup contains a balance of forms, an asymmetrical juxtaposition of plants, water, rock, and other natural elements. The way in which these forms relate to each other alters as one moves along the garden's meandering paths. Stately trees, ferns, water lilies, irises, wildflowers, terraces, streams, and waterfalls seem to be in perfect harmony, as if ordered by nature.

After Walter Beck's death in 1954, Lester Collins, once chairman of the Department of Landscape Architecture at Harvard, and a colleague of Beck's, continued the development of the garden. He is now president of Innisfree Foundation, Inc.

Stone slab "sculptures" reflect Innisfree's Chinese design inspiration.

INSTITUTE OF ECOSYSTEM STUDIES, MARY FLAGLER CARY ARBORETUM
Millbrook

On property acquired by the New York Botanical Garden (see p. 75) in 1971, this research and education facility was established in the memory of Mary Flagler Cary, whose 2,000-acre estate the preserve now occupies. The 600 public-access acres of the site encompass the Institute of Ecosystem Studies, formed by the New York Botanical Garden in 1983 to "focus on ecological education and long-term study of disturbance and recovery in northern temperate ecosystems." Features of the site, demonstrating that environmental and ecological considerations need not be incompatible with eye-pleasing attractiveness, include: the Perennial Garden, emphasizing low maintenance and containing 800 different species and cultivars, one of the largest collections of such plants to be seen in a public garden in the northeast; the Fern Glen, displaying over 100 European and Asian varieties in an appropriate setting; the Howard Taylor Lilac Collection, featuring 69 varieties amid plantings of irises, daylilies, and balloon flowers; the Meadow Garden, showcasing little bluestem grass as a practical and attractive groundcover; and the Greenhouse, where tropicals are displayed and propagation techniques are demonstrated.

Major tree collections comprising the arboretum include pines, birches, and willows, and nature trails on the property examine a number of habitats, including forests, marshes, fields, thickets, and stream banks. The Gifford House, built as a private home in 1817, is the site of the Education Program's classes and workshops, as well as a gift and plant shop.

Cary Arboretum combines pink echinacea, golden rudbeckia, and sedum.

Gray and green santolinas, begonias, and Joseph's coat in a Mohonk mosaic.

MOHONK MOUNTAIN HOUSE
New Paltz

Mohonk Mountain House, perched on a rocky ledge overlooking Lake Mohonk in the Shawangunk Mountains, began as a small boardinghouse in 1870. Its Quaker proprietors, twin brothers Albert and Alfred Smiley, had purchased 300 acres of the picturesque, rugged terrain surrounding the 40-room house. They immediately set about renovating and expanding the original structure, and by the turn of the century it had grown to what it is today—a one-eighth-of-a-mile-long building with towers and gables and room enough for up to 500 guests.

The natural beauty and spectacular vistas of the grounds of Mohonk remain for present-day visitors virtually unspoiled from the time they were enjoyed by Victorian visitors more than 100 years ago. The resort is especially noted for its rustic twig-and-bough structures. These include more than 100 gazebos, or summer houses, some laden with wisteria, strategically placed throughout the property to afford the best views of the surrounding scenery.

The approximately 15 acres of cultivated gardens were begun by Albert Smiley in 1886, and ever since, the resort has had a history of horticultural excellence. Paths wander through vine-covered arbors to discover: a rose garden; perennial borders; a Show Garden with beds of annuals, biennials, and perennials; an herb garden; a greenhouse open to visitors; and a wildflower and fern trail with more than 30 different kinds of ferns, mostly native to the area, and well over 100 varieties of wildflowers and woodland plants.

In the last 20 years, more than 100 new varieties of trees and shrubs have been added to those already established. These include such favorites as deutzias, viburnums, shrub honeysuckles, mock oranges, old-fashioned lilacs, weigelas, spireas, and hydrangeas.

NEW YORK CITY

THE NEW YORK BOTANICAL GARDEN
Bronx

One of America's premier botanic gardens in terms of its dynamic academic and scientific tradition and leadership, the New York Botanical Garden (NYBG) occupies a verdant 250-acre preserve in the heart of the Bronx's urban sprawl. Nathaniel Lord Britton, one of the founders of the garden in 1891, intended it to echo the likes of the celebrated 1844 Palm House at the Royal Botanic Gardens at Kew in London. Indeed, the Enid A. Haupt Conservatory, the NYBG's crowning jewel, rivals the great glass house at Kew in size and beauty. Completed in 1901 and entirely rebuilt in

The Haupt Conservatory's central dome at The New York Botanical Garden.

1978, the structure features a 90-foot-high and 100-foot-in-diameter central dome and outreaching wings that cover a total of 44,000 square feet of seasonal displays and permanent collections. Among the latter are the Palm Grove under the dome, Tropicals, Subtropicals, the Old World Desert, the American Desert, and the Fern Forest, enveloping a waterfall and a pool.

The sprawling grounds, dotted with mature specimen trees amid expanses of lawn in the English manner, encompass: a Pinetum; an Herb Garden; a Rock Garden, with a replicated alpine setting; a Native Plant Garden, containing a spring-fed marsh and a New Jersey pine barrens setting; a Rose Garden, featuring handsome metal latticework; and home Demonstration Gardens. The forest preserve occupying the remaining 40 acres represents New York City's last piece of untouched woodland.

Designed in 1896 by Robert W. Gibson, the Museum Building presides imposingly over the grounds, while housing administrative offices, classrooms, a 100,000-volume library, and the NYBG's renowned herbarium. The institution's extensive educational program encompasses all areas of botany, horticulture, ecology, and landscape design, with courses designed for professionals, as well as nonprofessional adults and children.

The NYBG was incorporated in 1891, and land in Bronx Park was set aside for it by the city, with the proviso that $250,000 be raised. With the likes of J. Pierpont Morgan, Cornelius Vanderbilt II, and Andrew Carnegie on the garden's Board of Managers, the funds were soon appropriated.

WAVE HILL
Bronx

A grand old estate that Toscanini rented when he was conducting the NBC Symphony, 28-acre Wave Hill occupies a spectacular site overlooking the mighty Hudson River and the cliffs of the New Jersey Palisades on its opposite shore. Built in 1843, Wave Hill House was acquired in 1893 by wealthy financier George Perkins who laid out and developed the gardens and added Glyndor, another manor house on the property. The site remained under private ownership until 1960 when it was given to the City of New York.

Dedicated to horticultural excellence and education, the grounds today are a series of sumptuous gardens populated with an amazing variety of plants, many rare and unusual kinds among them. Major points of interest include a Flower Garden, an Herb Garden, an English-style Wild Garden, an Aquatic Garden, a Thematic Plant Exhibit, and an Alpine House. A 2,000-square-foot conservatory shelters seasonal floral displays and collections of truly exotic tropicals, cacti, and succulents.

As a "public, nonprofit institution committed to examining and interpreting the complex interaction between human beings and the natural world," the facility features workshops and educational programs for both children and adults. The Wave Hill Learning Center is an interactive museum offering discovery boxes, murals and maps, hands-on exhibits, aquaria, and a model of the Hudson shoreline. Wave Hill is owned by the City of New York, and receives a portion of its support in public funds through the New York City Department of Cultural Affairs. The property is managed by Wave Hill, Inc., formed in 1965.

Pink schizanthus turns Wave Hill's conservatory into a spring showcase.

BROOKLYN BOTANIC GARDEN
Brooklyn

The unique charm and Gardenesque grandeur of the Brooklyn Botanic Garden have occupied an indelible place in my consciousness as far back as I can remember. Before I could walk, my mother wheeled me in a stroller through its verdant 52 acres. And ever since a group of horticulturally-minded citizens established it in 1910 on a former city dump site, it has served as an emerald oasis of recreation, inspiration, and education for millions of New Yorkers, as well as visitors from every corner of the world.

Wandering among BBG's series of formal and naturalized settings, one is immediately reminded of the great estate gardens of Europe, with the historic-landmark Administration Building, designed by McKim, Mead and White in Italian-Renaissance style, presiding like a manor house over the garden's grand plan. In early spring, visitors approaching the building's main entrance are treated to Magnolia Plaza's unprecedented profusion of assorted species of the miraculous tree-borne blooms. Off to one side of the Plaza is BBG's famous Japanese Hill-and-Pond-Garden. Designed in 1915 by Takeo Shiota replete with teahouse, waterfall, gate-of-heaven, and Shinto temple, it is one of the finest examples in the Western hemisphere of age-old, traditional Japanese landscape design. Also not to be missed is the Cranford Rose Garden, a storybook formal design, with latticework pavilion, incorporating over 5,000 bushes in peak bloom in early June.

Fiery trees and euonymus hedges ignite Brooklyn Botanic Garden in fall.

Other outstanding features include: Cherry Esplanade, a grand allee of Japanese Kwanzan cherry trees, in full bloom in late April; the Rock Garden; Herb Garden; Rhododendron Garden; Osborne Memorial Section, ablaze with azaleas in early spring; Local Flora Section, containing plants native to the area within a 100-mile radius of New York City; Shakespeare Garden; Fragrance Garden for the Blind; and the Children's Garden, bursting forth in summer with vegetables and flowers grown by hundreds of children each year.

BBG was a pioneer in horticultural education, having, at its inception, established the world's first hands-on learning garden for children and a training program for schoolteachers. Continuing that tradition today are its summer children's program, its courses and lectures for adults, and its quarterly *Plants & Gardens* handbooks which have dispensed timely gardening information throughout the world for almost half a century.

The latter-day addition of the Steinhardt Conservatory propelled the garden into the twenty-first century. Completed in 1988 at a cost of 26 million dollars, it encompasses three space-age glass houses installed with tropical, desert, and temperate collections of plants in naturalized, walk-through settings. The construction project also included new classroom facilities and a space for displaying BBG's celebrated collection of priceless bonsai.

QUEENS BOTANICAL GARDEN
Flushing

A 26-acre greenery and floral oases holding its own against a near-explosive urban surround, this garden is one of the treasured New York City institutions providing ever more vital sanctuary from the increasing noise, congestion, and air pollution endured by all of us New Yorkers. Serving its immediate neighborhood in Flushing, in the borough of Queens, as well as visitors from far and wide, the facility began as a five-acre exhibit at the 1939–1940 New York World's Fair. During the war, its plantings remained unused and forgotten. But in 1946, with the encouragement of then-Parks Commissioner Robert Moses, a group of civic-minded citizens formed the Queens Botanical Garden Society, with the

A wedding gazebo ornaments Queens Botanical Garden's rose garden.

aim of restoring the site as a public garden, as well as establishing it as a center of horticultural information and education for the people of Queens. By 1960 the facility had been enlarged to 20 acres, but with a 1964 World's Fair on the horizon, the garden was forced once again to take stock of its situation. Having to make way for the international exposition, it was relocated to a new site suggested by Mr. Moses. At its present location since 1963, the facility has grown into a major cultural and educational institution serving a community of well over two million people.

The rambling, tree-studded landscape, negating all evidence of the city's hustle and bustle, features colorful floral displays that are changed three times during the year. Spring is celebrated with massive plantings of more than 80,000 tulips, and these are replaced with annuals in summer and chrysanthemums in fall. The Charles H. Perkins Memorial Rose Garden, one of the largest in the Northeast, displays all kinds of old as well as hybrid varieties.

Six demonstration gardens offer innovative ideas for the amateur gardener, while six teaching gardens serve as living laboratories for the extensive horticultural programs offered to children and adults by the garden's Department of Education. These installations number: the Bird Garden, featuring plants that provide our feathered friends with food, shelter, and nesting material; the Bee Garden, with a working hive and planted with the kinds of nectar-laden flowers bees are attracted to; the Ethnic Garden, exhibiting plants used by people around the world and organized according to continent of origin; the Herb Garden, containing a selection of aromatic, culinary, pigmentary, and medicinal herbs; the Woodland Garden, including a waterfall, a pool, both native and introduced tree varieties, and an extensive collection of ferns and ericaceous specimens; and the Pinetum, a collection of conifer species and their varieties.

The garden is a quasi-municipal corporation, funded in part by the City of New York, under the jurisdiction of the Department of Cultural Affairs, and in part by private donations and membership.

THE CENTRAL PARK CONSERVATORY GARDEN
Manhattan

Way up in northern Central Park, on its eastern perimeter near 105th Street, lies a treasure yet to be discovered by most Manhattanites. Ornately majestic wrought-iron gates announce the entrance to an otherworldly garden, the only one of classic, formal design anywhere in the park. The stylized plants depicted in the metal of the gates hint at the wonders that lie within and pique the curiosity of passersby along Fifth Avenue. Crafted in Paris in 1894 for the Vanderbilt mansion that once occupied a site on Fifth Avenue some 50 blocks to the south, the gates were spared demolition, and were bequeathed to the city in 1939.

Spring crab apple blooms glorify the Conservatory Garden's center section.

Covering about six acres in all, the Conservatory Garden is made up of three basic areas. The largest, the Central Garden, is bordered on the north and south by two smaller gardens. Once through the Vanderbilt Gate, the visitor commands a breathtaking view of the half-acre, rectangular greensward, edged with yew hedges, that dominates the Central Garden. Flanking this open space are double allees of crab apples, billowing with clouds of bloom in early spring, and at its far end, beyond a fountain, is a spectacular metal-latticework pergola supporting the twisted trunks of 50-year-old wisteria vines. Having a special interest in garden architecture, particularly latticework of all kinds, I was delighted to find this ornate example, probably one of the grandest in the city.

In the North Garden, designed in the round, planting beds encircle the Untermyer Fountain, the creation of Walter Schott. Nearest it are French-style parterre beds, with santolina planted in scroll-shape designs and surrounded by seasonal annuals. Moving outward from the fountain, the next circle of beds boasts 20,000 tulips in spring and 5,000 chrysanthemum plants bursting with bloom in the fall. Each of the four paths leading from this garden takes the visitor through a charming arbor archway, festooned in June with the white flowers of an old-fashioned climbing rose, 'Silver Moon.'

The South Garden is dominated by a Bessie Porter Vonnoh sculpture depicting two children in a favorite book of mine, *The Secret Garden*, the young people's classic by Frances Hodgson Burnett. In summer, tropical water lilies occupy the pool surrounding the statue. Otherwise, this garden, also known as The Secret Garden, is notable for its English-style herbaceous borders spilling over with masses of perennials, more than 175 different kinds. The borders were designed to provide year-round interest, with foliage texture and color contributing to the overall composition.

The Conservatory Garden takes its name from the complex of Victorian glass houses that occupied its site from 1899 to 1934. A popular attraction in the early 1900s, this facility supplied plants for parks throughout the city. It was razed by Parks Commissioner Robert Moses to make way for a new garden under the auspices of the W.P.A., to provide employment during the Depression. With planting plans by M. Betty Sprout and landscaping by Gilmore D. Clarke, the garden that opened in 1937 was popular with the surrounding community. But by the 1960s, it had fallen into terrible disrepair, and in the late 1970s, the New York Committee of the Garden Club of America began reviving the plantings and raising funds for repair of the fountains. Thanks to a sizable grant from Rockefeller Center, major restoration efforts began in earnest in 1982 under the combined efforts of the Central Park Conservancy and the City of New York Department of Parks and Recreation. A 1.5 million-dollar endowment from the Weiler-Arnow family in 1987 insured the garden's preservation.

Much of the credit for its incomparable beauty must be given to its present-day director, Lynden B. Miller, an artist and horticulturist who redesigned all of the beds with an expert eye toward juxtaposing plant colors, textures, and conformations.

THE CLOISTERS
Manhattan

Housing the Metropolitan Museum's collection of medieval art, The Cloisters sits majestically on a bluff overlooking the Hudson River, just north of the George Washington Bridge. Replicating the austerity of medieval archi-

The Trie Cloister, one of The Cloisters' three courtyard gardens.

tecture, the single structure incorporates sections of a 12th-century chapterhouse, the cloisters of five monasteries, and a Romanesque chapel. Three fascinating and informative courtyard gardens are installed with plants grown in western Europe during the Middle Ages (800 to 1520 A.D.). The Cuxa Cloister Garth Garden features fragrant plants, and the Bonnefont Cloister Herb Garden, containing 250 species in raised beds, is installed with wattle fences and a wellhead. The Trie Cloister Garden contains all of the plants depicted in the seven Hunt of the Unicorn Tapestries, one of the museum's most celebrated acquisitions.

The unique structure and the art it contains were funded by John D. Rockefeller, Jr. Opened to the public in 1938, the Cloisters hosts a full program of lectures, concerts, and special events throughout the year.

The formal walled garden is among Old Westbury Gardens' major attractions.

OLD WESTBURY GARDENS
Old Westbury

One of the last remaining of the grand old Long Island estates that inspired Fitzgerald's *The Great Gatsby*, Old Westbury House and Gardens are recognizable to many from the endless numbers of films—among them, *Love Story*—and commercials that have made use of their unparalleled beauty. No matter how many times I drive up the long allee of old lindens that marks the impressive entrance and catch my first glimpse of the house, I am reminded once again of the impeccable sense of aesthetics that reigns over this majestic homestead. From the grandest gesture to the smallest detail, there is not a single lapse in taste.

Built in 1906 for John Shaffer Phipps, the son of steel magnate Henry Phipps, both the house and gardens were designed by the London-born architect George A. Crawley. To please his new wife, Margarita, an English aristocrat, John Phipps commissioned a manor house typical of those built in England during the reign of Charles II in the seventeenth century. True to his patron, Crawley designed a showplace in which classical symmetry and sumptuous vistas abounded. These remain intact today. In fact, since 1959 when the Phipps family established a foundation to oversee the estate and open it to the public, it has been preserved inside and out exactly as it might have appeared more than 75 years ago.

The 72-room mansion is filled with English antiques from the eighteenth century and earlier and paintings by Reynolds, Constable, Gainsborough, and Sargent, among others. Through the French doors and out onto the terrace at the back of the house, the visitor is beckoned into the gardens by a long axis that seems to disappear into the horizon. Off this axis are a sunken rose garden in the round and an Italianate walled garden, the most abundantly floral of all. Of formal design, this garden in summer offers borders spilling over with a wide assortment of annuals and perennials. Crowning the plan at its far end are three elaborate lattice pavilions. Connected by a curving colonnade, these offer sturdy support for bowers of wisteria blossoms in spring.

Also to be found among the grounds' 100 acres are: woodland paths, a wildflower meadow, a thatched cottage scaled for children and planted with foxgloves and delphiniums, a temple of love overlooking a lake, a boxwood garden, a lilac garden, and demonstration gardens offering ideas for homeowners.

A lead container sports chrysanthemums in a Planting Fields greenhouse.

PLANTING FIELDS ARBORETUM
Oyster Bay

The former estate of William Coe, Planting Fields today is a 400-acre treasure trove of horticultural splendors. Containing more than 6,500 kinds of plants, the site is renowned for its spectacular displays of thousands (800 species) of rhododendrons and azaleas, aflame with bloom from April to June. Flowering cherries, crab apples, dogwoods, and magnolias add their own clouds of blossoms to turn the estate into a springtime floral festival.

Reflecting the British roots of Mr. Coe, who came to this country at the age of 14 from Worcestershire, England, the estate's manor house, built in 1918 and containing 75 rooms, is one of the finest examples in America of Elizabethan architecture. The grounds also, designed with the help of the famous Olmsted brothers, recall the style of a traditional English country estate, with broad, sweeping lawns punctuated by large specimen trees.

The property's camellia greenhouse contains over 100 varieties, and the remainder of the greenhouse complex hosts a permanent orchid collection and floral displays, including a fall Chrysanthemum Show, that are changed six times each year. The five-acre Synoptic Garden, a collection of shrubs arranged alphabetically, contains over 400 exceptional species and cultivars. Other must-see areas are the formal Italian Garden, adrift with wisteria and lilacs in spring, the Dwarf Conifer Garden, and the Wildflower Garden. During summer, the grounds are enlivened with plantings of annuals.

Upon his death in 1955, William Coe's horticultural showplace was bequeathed to the people of New York State. Today, the estate is registered as a Historic District and is administered by the Long Island State Park Commission. Planting Fields offers an extensive program of short courses, and contains an outstanding horticultural library and an herbarium with 10,000 pressed specimens.

HIGHLAND BOTANICAL PARK
Rochester

Designed by America's preeminent landscaper, Frederick Law Olmsted, Highland Park bears his unmistakable signature: broad greenswards crowned with stately specimen trees and cut with winding paths and carriage drives. In the late nineteenth century, it was the dream of George Ellwanger and Patrick Barry, owners of Mt. Hope Nurseries, to bring some of the benefits of the countryside to Rochester's urban residents. They donated 20 acres of their nursery grounds and their choicest stock toward the creation of a park, and in 1888 the Rochester Park Commission dedicated Highland as the city's first.

Chosen to design the tract, Olmsted planted its hillsides with hundreds of trees and shrubs to create a setting that looked natural and unplanned. As it matured through the years, talented horticulturists furthered the dreams of Olmsted, Ellwanger, and Barry by seeking rare and unusual plants from around the world to establish the park's status as an arboretum. Indeed, in an effort to equal the collections of Harvard's Arnold Arboretum (see p. 37)—also designed by Olmsted—there was an active exchange of plant material between the two institutions.

John Dunbar planted the grounds' first lilacs in 1892, and during his tenure as the park's chief horticulturist, he gradually expanded the collection, introducing more than 30 new varieties to the trade. The deep sky-blue 'President Lincoln', a 1916 Dunbar introduction, is still considered to be the best of the blue lilacs. Dunbar's successor, Bernard H. Slavin, continued the additions, and today Highland can boast the largest display in the world, covering 22 acres and numbering 1,200 shrubs of more than 500 varieties. Starting the third week of every May, a ten-day lilac festival attracts devotees from far and wide. 'Rochester', a creamy white variety introduced in 1963, commemorates the city's lilac heritage.

Other major collections to be found at Highland are horse chestnuts, magnolias, barberries, Japanese maples, and rhododendrons. In addition to scores of rare, noteworthy, and flowering trees, the grounds are dotted with boxwood, forsythia, spirea, weigela, witch hazel, and yew, and encompass a rock garden, featuring dwarf evergreens, a pinetum, and a pansy bed, with 10,000 plants installed in a different floral-carpet pattern each year.

The Lambert Conservatory, a landmark since 1911, houses five seasonal floral displays throughout the year, plus permanent exhibits of tropical and desert plants. The Garden Center of Rochester, occupying the park's historic Warner Castle (1854), collects and disseminates horticultural information. Its facilities include a library and nine specialty gardens.

Lilac time sparks a community celebration at Highland Botanical Park.

A storybook Victorian manse presides over the sprawling grounds of Lyndhurst.

LYNDHURST
Tarrytown

On the east bank of the Hudson, just south of the Tappan Zee Bridge's seemingly endless span, sits one of the grandest of the string of mansions built along the mighty waterway from New York to Albany during the time of the Hudson River Valley painters. One of the country's finest examples of Gothic-Revival architecture, Lyndhurst is all stone turrets, gables, and pointed arches. It was designed in 1838 by Alexander Jackson Davis for New York City mayor William Paulding, and was subsequently the residence of merchant George Merritt. In 1865 the architect doubled the size of the house for its new owner, railroad tycoon Jay Gould, who loved escaping the pressures of the city and enjoying the company of his family at the country estate. After Gould's death, Lyndhurst was maintained in turn by his daughters Helen and Anna, until 1961 when it was given to the National Trust for Historic Preservation, a nonprofit organization that oversees 16 historic houses nationwide through membership support.

The grounds' 67 acres are typical of the picturesque landscapes made popular in 1840s America by Andrew Jackson Downing. His signature is seen in the sweeping greenswards dotted with specimen spruces, dogwoods, magnolias, Japanese maples, and in the curving driveway that gradually reveals the estate in "surprise" views. A rockery, a rose garden with 127 varieties, a children's playhouse, a wrought-iron garden pavilion, and a greenhouse (the first with metal framing and the largest of its kind when built in 1881) sustain the manor's Victorian Gothic motif.

PENNSYLVANIA

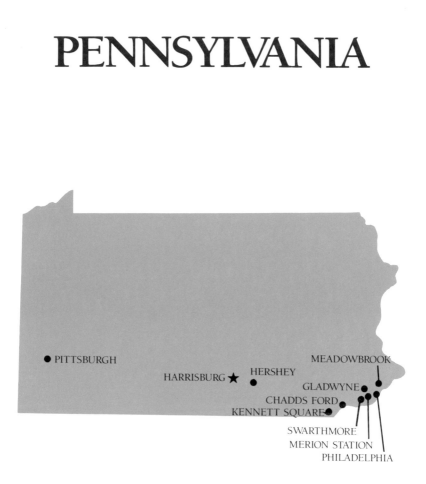

PITTSBURGH

MEADOWBROOK

HARRISBURG ★ HERSHEY

GLADWYNE

CHADDS FORD

KENNETT SQUARE

SWARTHMORE
MERION STATION
PHILADELPHIA

BRANDYWINE RIVER MUSEUM
Chadds Ford

The Wildflower and Native Plant Garden that surrounds the Brandywine River Museum was started in 1974 and dedicated by Lady Bird Johnson in 1979. Designed by FM Mooberry, the grounds contain three acres of gardens and 25 acres of meadow, with more than 300 species of plants.

The bucolic setting of the meandering Brandywine River forms the perfect backdrop for this showcase of wildflowers and native trees and shrubs, an eloquent argument in favor of their versatility and appropriateness for the home landscape. From spring's first bloodroot to fall's last bluestem goldenrod, wildflowers of all kinds fill borders and line walkways at this institution. And other indigenous plants offer a feel for the vanishing Brandywine countryside, a constant source of inspiration for artists.

The works of these artists may be appreciated in the museum, a restored 100-year-old grist mill that houses American illustration, still lifes, landscapes, particularly those of the Brandywine Valley, and paintings by members of the celebrated Wyeth family. Seeds for the wildflowers seen outdoors may be purchased in the museum gift shop.

A wave of evening primrose beautifies Brandywine River Museum.

Lilies number among the Henry's outstanding collection of plants.

HENRY FOUNDATION FOR BOTANICAL RESEARCH
Gladwyne

The Henry Foundation for Botanical Research, a 40-acre preserve of valued American native plants, is the legacy of Mary G. Henry, its founder. During 40 years of travel throughout the country, this intrepid plant hunter gathered countless rare specimens to insure their survival and dissemination.

Outstanding collections of magnolias, halesias, rhododendrons, azaleas, styrax, liliums, vacciniums, chionanthus, and ilex alternate with rock outcroppings in this hilly, naturalized setting. Best times for color are April and May, when the rhododendrons and azaleas are in bloom and September and October, when the perennials and fall foliage are in top performance.

HERSHEY GARDENS
Hershey

In the span of a half century, the Hershey Gardens have blossomed from a 3½-acre rose plot to a magnificent 23-acre sweeping display of seasonal flowers, specimen trees and shrubs, theme gardens, and 8,000 rosebushes representing some 450 varieties. In 1936 Dr. J. Horace McFarland asked his good friend Milton S. Hershey of chocolate fame to donate a million dollars toward the establishment of a national rosarium near Washington, D.C. Instead, Hershey decided to create a garden in his hometown, and in 1937 Hershey Rose Gardens opened to the public, attracting nearly 20,000 visitors in a single day. By 1941, the installation had expanded to its full 23 acres to include tulips, annuals, and such specimen trees as a giant sequoia, blue atlas cedar, bald cypress, oriental spruce, and copper beech. By the 1960s, collections of dwarf and weeping conifers and evergreens, hollies, rhododendrons, azaleas, sedums and sempervivums, Japanese maples, and unusual flowering shrubs had joined the ranks, elevating the facility to near botanic-garden significance.

Hershey Gardens features drifts of spring tulips, hyacinths, and daffodils.

By 1979 the last major additions had been completed. These constituted six theme gardens, each an expression of a particular design style: the Japanese Garden, the Henry J. Hohman Garden of Hollies and Dwarf Evergreens, the Original Rose Garden, the Garden of Ornamental Grasses, the Garden of Old Roses, and the Garden of Shrubs for Summer Interest. Laid out in comfortable succession to one another, these are offset in spring by some 30,000 tulips, along with crocuses, irises, daffodils, fritillaria, and the billowing bloom of cherry, dogwood, magnolia, and crab apple trees. Rhododendrons, azaleas, and peonies (100 varieties) burst with color from mid-May to early June. Annuals, planted in numbers totalling

9,000, are at their peak by early July and remain in bloom until mid-September. Augmenting the summer display is a geranium test area containing 100 varieties, and fall is celebrated with the planting of some 2,000 chrysanthemums.

The gardens, now under the operation and administration of the M. S. Hershey Foundation, were named an All-America Rose Selections test site in 1988. Also, within their vicinity the Hershey Food Corporation presents a zoo, the Hershey Museum of American Life, and Chocolate World.

LONGWOOD GARDENS
Kennett Square

The undisputed flagship of America's botanic gardens, Longwood encompasses 1,000 acres, of which 350 are devoted to outdoor gardens of every kind and description. The revered institution boasts 3½ acres under glass in its spectacular high-ceilinged conservatories, plus 20 greenhouses exhibiting all kinds of rare and exotic insectivorous plants, orchids, aquatics, tropicals, and cacti and succulents. In all, the facility displays some 11,000 kinds of plants indoors and out.

The Pierce-du Pont House on the grounds dates from 1730, and descendents of the Pierce family planted the property's oldest trees. The grounds were already a local attraction in the early 1800s, but it was not until 1906, when Pierre S. du Pont, who would become chairman of the Du Pont Company as well as General Motors, purchased the site to save the trees, that Longwood began to be developed into what it is today. Pierre was a cousin of the creators of Nemours (see p. 25) and Winterthur (see p. 27) and the great-grandson of the master of Eleutherian Mills (see p. 23). Starting construction of the massive conservatory structures in 1918, du Pont opened them to the public in 1921.

Poinsettias celebrate the Christmas season in a conservatory at Longwood.

Outstanding features number: the conservatories, with landscaped gardens and spectacular seasonal displays (on my first visit, during the fall, I had never seen anything like the huge spheres of cascading chrysanthemums that were suspended from the beams of the glass ceiling, and was truly awe-struck by the magnitude of the display); Flower Garden Walk; Hillside Garden; Italian Water Garden; Topiary Garden; Idea Garden; the extravagant fountains and pools and their illuminated evening shows; and one of the world's largest pipe organs, housed within the conservatory complex. In addition to chrysanthemums, seasonal spectaculars include poinsettias and lighted trees at Christmas, and summertime tropical water lilies, some with pads 10 feet in diameter and able to support the weight of a man.

Longwood offers a full program of lectures and courses, and, in association with the University of Delaware, a two-year graduate internship in ornamental horticulture.

Structure and ornament of classic mien define Meadowbrook's formal "rooms."

MEADOWBROOK FARM
Meadowbrook

Meadowbrook Farm is the labor of love of J. Liddon Pennock, Jr., past president of the Pennsylvania Horticultural Society (see p. 95) and a man of great taste and vision whose exhibits at the Philadelphia Flower Show always set new standards of beauty and horticultural showmanship. His commercial greenhouse establishment specializes in the sale of ferns, cacti and other succulents, orchids, begonias, topiaries of all forms and sizes, and garden statuary and ornaments of impeccable proportion. Beckoning buyers outdoors in summer is a wide assortment of trees, shrubs, annuals, and more than 600 varieties of perennials and ornamental grasses.

But the ultimate embodiment of Mr. Pennock's exceptional eye for design is his own private garden, sequestered in a nearby portion of the estate and open to groups of no less than 15 by appointment only. An enchanting series of 20 small formal gardens promotes the feeling of strolling through a mansion of lovely green rooms, each gently contributing to, yet yielding to the next. Framed by gazebos, belvederes, pools, fountains, stairways, walls, topiaries, espaliers, and allees, the terraced gardens offer a textbook summary of seemingly endless traditional design possibilities. The illusion of grandness defies the visitor to believe that the whole occupies no more than one acre. The reward of more than 40 years of Mr. and Mrs. Pennock's dedication, the gardens abound with gardenias, hibiscus, oleanders, annuals, perennials, ivies, and a variety of flowering vines.

ARBORETUM OF THE BARNES FOUNDATION
Merion Station

Since 1940, the Arboretum School of the Barnes Foundation has offered courses in botany, horticulture, and landscape architecture principally for the betterment of the home gardener. The 12 acres of land associated with it is in essence its laboratory-classroom. As such, an amazingly large and diverse number of tree and shrub specimens and specialty gardens are squeezed into a manageably small confine for the edification of students, as well as interested visitors. Plentifully represented are a variety of species of lilac, maple, holly, oak, and viburnum, and splendidly mature specimens of rare varieties. The facility also includes a woodland tract, collections of dwarf conifers and woody vines, and peony, rose, rock, and heath gardens. Ferns and wildflowers add a finishing touch to the setting.

The land containing the arboretum had been part of the estate of Joseph Lapsley Wilson until it was purchased by Dr. Albert C. Barnes in 1922.

A number of lilac species may be compared at the Barnes Foundation.

Wilson stipulated as part of the sale that the trees he had planted around 1887 be preserved. The arboretum began taking shape when Mrs. Laura L. Barnes added ferns and wildflowers and new trees and shrubs to the Wilson plantings.

The Barnes Foundation received its charter as an educational institution in 1922, and the arboretum was extended to its present size in 1933. The grounds' original estate house is now home to the Barnes Foundation Art Department and Gallery.

BARTRAM'S GARDEN
Philadelphia

Located on the Schuylkill River in Southwest Philadelphia, Bartram's Garden is an ideal place to learn about early Colonial horticulture and lifestyles. Begun in 1728 by John Bartram (1699–1777), a Quaker farmer and one of the most famous botanists and plant explorers of his day, the 27-acre garden contained the largest collection of native plants in all of Colonial America, constituting what could be called our first botanic garden. Bartram introduced Europe to some 200 new varieties, including the sugar maple, and today the garden reflects his passion for the unusual.

In addition to a medicinal and savory herb garden and a vegetable kitchen garden, the grounds contain some fascinating trees and shrubs, including Bartram oak (a hybrid of red and willow oaks), yellowwood, ginkgo, prickly ash, pawpaw, franklinia, mountain laurel, cucumber magnolia, hackberry, and *Ficus carica*. The homestead includes an eighteenth-century stone house with period furnishings, a barn, a stable, and other outbuildings.

The spring blooms of mountain laurel brighten Bartram's Garden.

John Bartram's descendants lived at the site and ran the garden as a nursery until 1850. The city of Philadelphia was persuaded to buy it for the development of a park in 1891, and in 1893 the descendants of Bartram formed the John Bartram Association to ensure the house and garden's preservation. It sponsors ongoing restoration of the house and gardens and a variety of research and educational programs related to Colonial American life. Its efforts depend on membership support.

MORRIS ARBORETUM OF THE
UNIVERSITY OF PENNSYLVANIA
Philadelphia

Listed on the National Register of Historic Places, the 92-acre Morris Arboretum encompasses a romantically beautiful landscape embellished with a Victorian temple, a hidden grotto, a swan pond, two Japanese gardens, and a sculpture garden. Its rolling hills, meadows, and woodlands were originally the 1887 estate of siblings John and Lydia T. Morris. Upon Lydia's death in 1932, the site was bequeathed to the University of

Pennsylvania as a public arboretum, as well as a center for research and education. With a collection of over 5,500 labeled trees and shrubs, the outdoor laboratory is laid out in a naturalistic style, with winding paths discovering streams, specialty gardens, and long, awe-inspiring vistas.

Horticultural high points include: the All-America Selections Rose Garden, featuring ideal varieties for the Philadelphia area; formal parterre flower beds; Oak Allee; and Azalea Meadow and Magnolia Slope, attracting thousands of visitors each spring to pay homage to their magnificent bloom. The notable tree collection, encompassing one of the most outstanding assemblages of Oriental varieties in the eastern United States, includes a number of rare specimens of stewartia, holly, Asian maple, viburnum, cherry, and witch hazel.

The facility's all-encompassing educational programs offer a variety of courses, workshops, and lectures, including a year-long internship for horticultural professionals and instruction in environmental and plant sciences for schoolteachers. Named the official arboretum of the commonwealth of Pennsylvania by the state legislature in 1988, the Morris promises peak bloom from April to June and vibrant color in the fall.

Swans and a temple abet the romanticism of the Morris Arboretum's snow-blanketed landscape.

THE PENNSYLVANIA HORTICULTURAL SOCIETY
Philadelphia

The Pennsylvania Horticultural Society is known to anyone in the gardening community as a leader in education and information and the sponsor of a colossal annual event, the Philadelphia Flower Show, the standard against which all others are measured. Founded in 1827, the society has brought its experience to bear on such programs as Philadelphia Green, encouraging gardens, street trees, and sitting parks, and the Harvest Show, a yearly gathering of exhibits and entertainment for plant enthusiasts.

Located in a restored Colonial building in Independence National Historical Park in Philadelphia, the society's headquarters boasts horticultural displays in its lobby, a 14,000-volume library, and an eighteenth-century-style garden on its grounds. Maintained by its members, the garden is laid out in three sections: formal parterres offering new plantings each spring, summer, and fall season; a small orchard; and a kitchen garden planted with vegetables, herbs and flowers for cutting. All of the varieties chosen are as closely related as possible to those grown by our Colonial forebears.

Begonias are among the annuals planted in the PHS headquarters garden.

'Electron' is a hybrid descendant of the old roses cherished at Wyck.

WYCK
Philadelphia

One of the oldest houses still standing in Philadelphia, Wyck was owned by nine generations of the same Quaker family from 1689 until 1973, when it was first opened to the public. The last family owner deeded the property to the Wyck Charitable Trust, and the gift included 2½ acres of land, the house and its contents, several outbuildings, a landscaped garden, and a small endowment. Each of the nine generations of family owners contributed something distinctive to the homestead, and the various additions, including an eighteenth-century smokehouse, an icehouse (1837), and a carriagehouse (1796), have given scholars and visitors alike a unique perspective on the development of Philadelphia, and America, from the seventeenth century to the present.

Under cultivation since the late eighteenth century, the garden, including fruit trees, wildflowers, wisteria, a variety of old and rare shrubs, a vegetable plot, and formal rose beds, is as significant a historical artifact as the buildings. The charming rose garden, with its box-bordered parterres, was first laid out in the 1820s by Jane Bowne Haines, who planted over 20 varieties of roses, some of which were first brought to America as early as 1750 and many of which still bloom today.

A rose is considered "old" if it was in cultivation by the middle of the nineteenth century, or at least before 1867, the year the first hybrid tea was introduced. Among the original roses planted by Jane are some truly treasured antiques, such as the apothecary rose, *Rosa gallica officinalis* (1500), believed to have been described by Pliny in the 1st century A.D., the Tuscany rose, *Rosa gallica* (ca. 1600), the cinnamon rose, *Rosa cinnamomea* 'Plena' (1500), and the cabbage rose, *Rosa centifolia* (ca. 1600), with its delicious old-fashioned fragrance. The generations that followed Jane continued the rose garden's cultivation, and today it is a living museum.

Included in the National Register of Historic Places, Wyck is strongly committed to a policy of maintenance and preservation of its facilities, and education regarding our American heritage.

PHIPPS CONSERVATORY
Pittsburgh

Funded by the scion of American steel, Henry Phipps, the Phipps Conservatory was the largest of its kind in the country when it was built in 1893. The majority of the exotic plants that graced the Columbian Exposition in Chicago found a new home in this structure in 1894, and amazingly, some of these may still be found in residence today. The sprawling 2½ acres under glass encompass 13 display houses with permanent collections of tropicals, especially orchids, a Japanese garden, and a Victorian aquatic garden. The Broderie Garden features seventeenth-century French-style parterre beds in all their intricate grandeur. Seasonal displays include a Fall Flower Show, featuring 400 varieties of chrysanthemums filling seven houses, a Christmas extravaganza, and a spring spectacular. In summer, beds of flowers and a tropical water-lily pond adorn the grounds immediately outside the conservatory. The facility is operated and maintained by the city's Department of Parks and Recreation.

Fragile cattleya orchids thrive in the warmth of the Phipps Conservatory.

PITTSBURGH CIVIC GARDEN CENTER
Pittsburgh

"Millionaire's Row" (Fifth Avenue) in Pittsburgh was once home to Richard Beatty Mellon and his wife, Jennie King Mellon. The couple occupied their palatial 65-room mansion, built in 1912, until Mrs. Mellon's death in 1938, when it was utilized by the American Red Cross, and then razed at the conclusion of the War. Fortunately for posterity, the Mellons' children, Richard and Cordelia, gave the estate's 13-acre grounds to the city of Pittsburgh to be maintained as a park in memory of their parents.

The Pittsburgh Civic Garden Center was begun in the 1930s by a group of citizens committed to stimulating interest and activity in horticulture, gardening, and the environment. The organization quickly outgrew its headquarters next to the Phipps Conservatory (see p. 97), and moved into the former carriagehouse at Mellon Park. The organization restored the grounds by installing a series of gardens that continue to reflect Mrs. Mellon's original vision: the Curto Educational Gardens, with ornamental plants not often used but recommended for Pennsylvania, encompass four color gardens, wildflowers, and perennial borders; the Groundcover Garden contains 70 varieties, plus a sampling of ornamental grasses; the Jennie King Mellon Garden, dedicated in 1980 and designed for low maintenance by landscape architect R. Jackson Seay, is planted with spring bulbs and summer annuals; the Herb Garden contains knot and Shakespeare gardens and old roses; the Dogwood Garden displays 12 tree and four shrub varieties; the Model Garden is reserved for trials of annuals; and the Rock Garden features alpines and dwarf evergreens tucked among boulders.

The city of Pittsburgh designated Mellon Park a Historic Landmark in 1982. The Garden Center receives no government funding, its activities being supported solely by membership, grants, and foundations.

A knot design in the Herb
Garden of the Pittsburgh
Civic Garden Center.

Topped by blue sage,
verbena spills over a pot
at Scott Arboretum.

SCOTT ARBORETUM
Swarthmore

Over 110 verdant acres of the Swarthmore College campus comprise the
Scott Arboretum, a rich selection of ornamental plants best suited to the
Delaware Valley. Established in 1929 by the family of Arthur Hoyt Scott as
a memorial to the 1895 Swarthmore graduate, the arboretum contains
5,000 different kinds of plants chosen for their ornamental quality, ease of
maintenance, and resistance to disease. Major categories include: flowering
cherries, corylopsis, crab apples, lilacs, magnolias, native azaleas, ornamental grasses, tree peonies, viburnums, wisteria, and witch hazels. Seasonal displays include spring-flowering bulbs, the Rose Garden, and the
Fragrant Garden.

The arboretum also provides facilities for three plant evaluation programs: the Styer Award under the aegis of the Pennsylvania Horticultural
Society; the Plant Introduction Scheme of the University of British Columbia Botanic Garden; and the National Crab Apple Evaluation Program.

RHODE ISLAND

★ PROVIDENCE

● BRISTOL

● PORTSMOUTH

● WYOMING

● NEWPORT

● WESTERLY

BLITHEWOLD GARDENS & ARBORETUM
Bristol

Designed in the style of a seventeenth-century English manor house, the mansion at Blithewold is a tribute to the gracious summer living of the wealthy in 1907 when it was built. Much of its architecture, decor, and furnishings have been preserved as a reflection of that bygone era, and the trees, shrubs, and flowers on the property have been maintained according to the original turn-of-the-century design of landscape architect John DeWolf. In addition to the rose, rock, and water gardens on the property, he planted numerous exotic trees and shrubs that are still not commonly grown in the Northeast. Among these were Chinese cedars, ginkgos, bamboos, a Chinese toon tree, and a giant sequoia that is now a stately specimen standing 85 feet tall, the largest of its kind east of the Rocky Mountains. The manor also encompasses a greenhouse, a cutting and vegetable garden, and a gazebo.

Blithewold was originally the residence of coal-mining magnate Augustus Van Wickle who gave it its name, taken from the middle English for "happy woodland." After his death, his widow, Bessie, and his daughter, Marjorie, took special interest in the gardens, overseeing their maintenance and opening them to garden clubs and other interested horticultural organizations. At Marjorie's death in 1976, Blithewold became the property of the Heritage Trust of Rhode Island, with the understanding that the beauty of its landscape would continue to be preserved for the enjoyment and education of the public.

An Oriental cherry endows Blithewold with shimmering springtime bloom.

NEWPORT MANSIONS
Newport

As the summering place of America's wealthiest families during La Belle Epoque at the turn of the century, Newport was celebrated as "the queen of American resorts." The industrial and financial scions of the time paid tribute to the sun, surf, and social ambience that drew them to this maritime community by building opulent "beach cottages" befitting their exalted statures. More than half a dozen of these remain today, maintained by The Preservation Society of Newport County. Established in 1945, this nonprofit, privately funded organization has made it possible for the public to appreciate an extraordinary cross section of America's rich architectural and horticultural heritage.

Spanning more than 150 years of interior and exterior design, New-port's preserved historic houses include: the Nichols-Wanton Hunter House (1748); Kingscote (1841), its exteriors bedecked with trellises and vines in a manner popular when it was built; Château-sur-Mer (1880), designed by Richard Morris Hunt, whose work helped change the face of Newport, as well as that of New York's Fifth Avenue; Marble House (1892), patterned by Hunt for William Kissam Vanderbilt after Versailles' Petit

A pergola crowns the parterre garden at Newport's The Breakers.

Green Animals sports topiaries in all kinds of humorous shapes.

Trianon, its grounds boasting an authentic Chinese teahouse; The Breakers (1893), Palladian in style, designed by Hunt for Cornelius Vanderbilt II, with second-floor interiors by Ogden Codman (see page 38), a man who also was instrumental in reviving elaborate latticework, or treillage, for American gardens; The Elms (1901), a copy of the Château d'Asnieres (1750) outside Paris, with grounds distinguished by statuary, fountains, gazebos, rhododendrons, enormous weeping beeches, and carefully pruned ginkgo, maple, and linden trees; and Rosecliff (1902), designed by Stanford White for the doyenne of Newport society, Theresa Fair Oelrichs, as a copy of Versailles' Grand Trianon, with a restored, five-bed formal rose garden and statuary by Augustus Saint-Gaudens.

Covering approximately a dozen acres, the gardens of the famous Breakers are particularly memorable. Designed by Ernest Bowditch, a student of Frederick Law Olmsted, the grounds include pin oaks, red maples, Japanese yews, Chinese junipers, and dwarf hemlocks. A parterre garden on one of the terraces was destroyed by a hurricane in 1938, but Bowditch's original pattern was reconstructed from old photographs, using pink and white alyssum and blue ageratum.

GREEN ANIMALS
Portsmouth

No gardening pursuit has given the world more entertaining wit and whimsy than the art of topiary. While it is serious in its demands of patient devotion and exactitude, the more frivolously comical its sculptural results, the better.

During a period that peaked about 300 years ago in England, topiary gardens were the pride and passion of kings and lesser lords of the manor. Many of their splendid collections survive to this day, one of which I had the privilege of seeing some years ago. Having been given an introduction to the late great designer and photographer Sir Cecil Beaton, I went to see him at his charming manor, Reddish House, in Broadchalk near Salisbury. I do not remember the house so much as I do the giant geometric-shape yew topiaries that stood guard in the garden. I was astounded when told that these were well over four centuries old.

Unfortunately, we do not have any that advanced in age on these shores, but we do have some splendid topiary gardens, precious few and rare as they may be, that are well worth making a special effort to see. One of the most outstanding of these is to be found in Portsmouth, Rhode Island. In 1872, Thomas E. Brayton, a cotton manufacturing company treasurer, purchased a summer residence there. The seven-acre property included a clapboard house, farm outbuildings, a vegetable garden, and a pasture. Brayton's gardener, Joseph Carreiro, had been trained in the art of topiary in his native Portugal, and since his employer was especially fascinated with this unusual form of gardening, the two worked together to build an extensive collection.

The 80 examples of topiary at Green Animals include 21 yew and California-privet animals and birds and 59 English-boxwood and California-privet geometric and ornamental shapes. The gardens they inhabit also contain roses, boxwood-edged formal flower beds, herbs, orchards, grape arbors, ponds with water lilies, and berry patches.

It was Brayton's daughter, Alice, who gave Green Animals its name. After her father's death in 1939, she made the estate her permanent residence and continued the work of developing the topiaries. Upon her death in 1974 at the age of 94, she left the entire complex to The Preservation Society of Newport County with the understanding that it would be permanently maintained and made accessible to the public.

Formal beds and a fountain dressed with cannas at Roger Williams Park.

ROGER WILLIAMS PARK
Providence

This 435-acre complex of horticultural and architectural attractions had its beginnings in 1871 when Betsey Williams bequeathed her 102-acre farm to the city of Providence in honor of its founder, her father Roger Williams. Landscape architect H.W.S. Cleveland transformed the farmland into a parklike setting of lakes, ponds, woodlands, and formal gardens. Through the 1890s the city expanded the facility 320 acres.

Included within the confines of the expansive preserve, now listed in the National Register of Historic Places, are a 1773 cottage (the birthplace of Betsey Williams) and such educational institutions as the Museum of Natural History and the Cormack Planetarium. The Zoo, the third oldest in the United States and specializing in endangered species preservation, features animals in naturalistic settings.

The four glass structures of the Charles H. Smith greenhouses contain a wealth of rare and exotic plants from around the world, and the outdoor Hartman Gardens, the Rose Garden, and the Japanese Garden are the largest among the specialty plantings scattered throughout the park. The Smith Greenhouses and the Hartman Gardens play host to three seasonal flower displays: poinsettias at Christmas, bulbs in the spring, and chrysanthemums in the fall.

SHAKESPEARE'S HEAD
Providence

This wonderful little garden is an unexpected surprise in the center of downtown Providence. Shakespeare's Head dates from 1772, when a sign depicting the head of the bard marked the establishment's exterior and gave it its name. The aged building was nearly lost forever when the city scheduled it for demolition in 1937, but was saved by a group of historically-minded citizens. In the subsequent process of clearing the grounds, evidence of an early garden scheme was uncovered. Guided by the outlines of the original beds, landscape architect James D. Graham prepared a plan for the garden's restoration. It was eventually realized by the Rhode Island Federation of Garden Clubs, which has maintained the plantings ever since.

Today, visitors have the privilege of rediscovering the charm of Colonial times in this delightful formal arrangement of crab apples and other old-fashioned flowering trees and shrubs, an herb garden, and beds of flowers surrounded by brick walkways. The setting's show of bloom is at its best in spring.

Crab apples contribute old-world charm to Shakespeare's Head.

WILCOX PARK
Westerly

Wilcox Park was born in 1898 when Mrs. Stephen Wilcox purchased a seven-acre estate and donated it to Westerly's Memorial and Library Association in honor of her late husband. Additional parcels were added until 1905 when the park's boundaries were established. Warren H. Manning, a former associate of Frederick Law Olmsted, designed a landscape for the original tract, incorporating its existing species in the planting scheme. Landscape architect Frank Hamilton continued this theme for the acreage acquired later.

In 1938 more than 100 mature trees fell victim to a devastating hurricane, and replanting efforts were begun immediately in an effort to recapture the former impact of the design. But beginning in the 1960s planting efforts began to shift gradually toward establishing a collection that would enhance the value of the park as an arboretum.

In addition to the many uncommon tree and shrub varieties planted to inspire their use in the home landscape, there are a number of outstanding gardens throughout the park that further its educational ideals: the Dwarf Conifer Garden, located in a rock-garden setting, is an excellent collection numbering 130 plants; the Herb Garden features annual and perennial kinds in a formal setting; hardy varieties specially chosen to provide color from spring until late fall dominate the Perennial Garden; and the Garden of the Senses, offering labels in braille, is composed of a 16-by-4-foot raised bed planted with species of distinctive flavor, texture, or fragrance. Other not-to-be-missed horticultural attractions include the Lily Pond, the Diane Howard Azalea Garden, and the Margaret Wise Brown Wildflower Collection.

Wilcox Park's stately trees glow with a rainbow of fall color.

Anise (Pimpinella anisum) *joins Meadowbrook's celebration of herbs.*

MEADOWBROOK HERB GARDEN
Wyoming

This commercial mail-order installation is noteworthy for the fact that all of its herbs and vegetables are grown organically. With great concern for and understanding of the environment and human constitutions, Thomas and Marjory Fortier, the owners of Meadowbrook, use no chemical fertilizers or pesticides on any of the plants grown at their facility. Visitors will find the operation's greenhouses and formal herb garden interesting and informative, and may purchase any of a wide variety of herbs packaged for culinary, tea, cosmetic, and medicinal uses. Workshops on herbs and their myriad applications are held throughout the summer, and a fair held every year at the end of May, promising enjoyment for the whole family, features bagpipers, maypole dancing, food, and lectures.

VERMONT

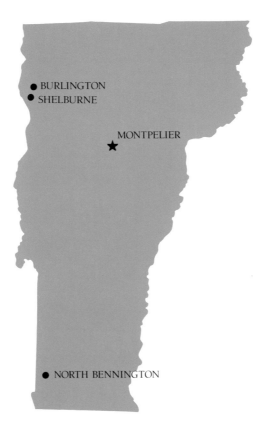

UNIVERSITY OF VERMONT AGRICULTURAL
EXPERIMENT STATION
Burlington

The research laboratory of the University of Vermont's College of Agriculture and Life Sciences, this 110-acre Experiment Station displays a wide variety of trees, shrubs, and flowering plants well suited to the climate of Vermont. Wonderful displays abound, including crab apples and other fruit trees, vegetables, lilacs and other flowering shrubs, and great stands of daylilies of all kinds. An official All-America Selections annual garden presents the latest and best introductions of bedding annuals, which seem to be regaining their popularity in the Northeast, after having been abandoned for some time in favor of perennials.

Established in 1887 through legislation introduced by Vermont Senator Justin Smith Morrill, the station's original charter was to improve agricultural practices through scientific investigation and experimentation. In more recent years, its focus has expanded to encompass all areas of gardening and the environment.

Lilacs comprise a major attraction at UV's Experiment Station.

THE PARK-MC CULLOUGH HOUSE
North Bennington

Dating from 1865, the Park-McCullough House offers an invitation to experience the ornate finery and elegant reserve of the Victorian era. Built by Trenor Park, a Bennington lawyer who made his fortune in California, and occupied for 100 years by members of the Park, Hall, and McCullough families, the 40-room summer "cottage" is an example of French Second Empire style. A commodious, all-encircling veranda looks out on sweeping lawns and aged trees, while inside, 14-foot ceilings and gas-fed bronze chandeliers preside over original furnishings, oak and walnut paneling, parquet floors, and marble mantels.

Vines clinging to trellises and flower-filled Victorian urns close by the house entice visitors to explore more of the grounds' charming delights: an annual and perennial Colonial garden, a grape arbor, herb and vegetable gardens, a greenhouse, a barn with family carriages and sleighs, and a children's playhouse, a scaled-down replica of the main structure.

Encompassing about six acres, the gardens were designed by Maud Hutchins in 1931, and have undergone considerable restoration in the years since. The estate is listed in the National Register of Historic Places.

Lavender is among the delights to be discovered at The Park-McCullough House.

SHELBURNE MUSEUM
Shelburne

This 45-acre preserve, encompassing 35 historic buildings, provides a rare glimpse of nineteenth-century American life. Founded in 1947 by Electra Havemeyer Webb to "show the craftsmanship and ingenuity of our fore-fathers," the restoration is Vermont's most popular tourist attraction. Like her parents, Mrs. Webb had a lifelong passion for collecting exceptional pieces of Americana, and the museum now contains a collection that is a very personal expression of this extraordinary woman's vision of American history and culture. Following her death in 1960, direction of the facility passed to her son, J. Watson Webb, Jr., who completed his mother's building plan and augmented and refined the site's many exhibits.

The beautifully manicured grounds include a culinary and dyeing herb garden in the front yard of the Hat and Fragrance Unit (ca. 1800), a medicinal herb garden as part of the Apothecary Shop, a rose garden, and the Pleissner Perennial Garden. Four hundred lilac bushes, encompassing almost 100 varieties, are in spectacular bloom in late May. Among the art collections found in the Webb Memorial Building are works by Rembrandt, Degas, Monet, and Manet. Native American artifacts are assembled in the Beach Gallery. Crafts demonstrations on the grounds are held at the 1840 Blacksmith and Wheelwright Shop, the Weaving Shed, and the Ben Lane Printing Shop.

Other attractions of interest to the whole family are: the Circus Building and its miniature parade and circus artifacts; an 1890 railroad station and private railroad car; a 1915 steam engine; a Toy Shop, with early examples;

an 1845 Covered Bridge; and the S.S. *Ticonderoga*, a National Historic Landmark and the last vertical-beam sidewheel steamship intact in the U.S. Furnished restored buildings include the 1733 Prentis House and the 1790 Stencil House, with its stenciled walls and painted furniture. A jitney transports visitors throughout the grounds and various shops offer books, prints, old-fashioned candy, and Vermont maple syrup among various other items.

The Shelburne is a nonprofit educational institution supported principally by admissions, sales, bequests, and contributions. Its Department of Education offers a variety of programs and special family events. Membership in the museum, open to all, includes free admission to the site and various other privileges.

Hybrid lupines, typical of the bloom found in Shelburne's perennial garden.

CANADA

NEWFOUNDLAND

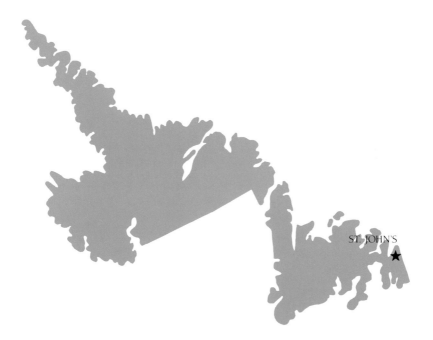

ST. JOHN'S ★

MEMORIAL UNIVERSITY BOTANICAL GARDEN
AT OXEN POND
St. John's

The Memorial University Botanical Garden is a rambling preserve of untamed natural wonders. With the aim of familiarizing visitors and students
with the flora and fauna of the heathlands, bogs and fens, fir forests, alder
thickets, rock outcroppings, and lake margins of the Newfoundland and
Labrador terrains, the university began developing a botanic park on three
acres of its grounds in 1971. Gradually expanding over the years, the
facility now covers 110 acres surrounding 12-acre Oxen Pond. With osprey
darting overhead and butterflies abounding, visitors wander along five
nature trails to investigate the habitats' riches, among them such wildflowers as the twinflower (*Linnaea borealis*) and bog laurel (*Kalmia poliifolia*
'Leucantha').

In addition to the wild areas, there are a number of gardens planted
with ornamentals to test their adaptability to the local climate and terrain.
These include: a perennial border; a woodland garden; heather beds; a
rock garden where 300 species and cultivars of exotics, dwarf shrubs, and
small bulbous plants are on trial; a cottage garden where a diversity of old-
fashioned blooms are grown in an attempt to mimic the traditional English
cottage garden and to attract butterflies and other pollinating insects; and a
Newfoundland heritage garden where annuals, biennials, and herbaceous
perennials traditionally grown in the area are planted, and where an example of an old-style natural-twig, or "Quiggly," fence, a fast-disappearing
rural standby, may be seen.

The university publishes a number of booklets concerning the wildlife,
environment, and specific gardening considerations of the Newfoundland
vicinity. A list of titles and prices is obtainable by writing.

*Butterflies surrender to
the lure of French
marigolds at Memorial.*

NOVA SCOTIA

ANNAPOLIS ROYAL HISTORIC GARDENS
Annapolis Royal

The ten-acre Annapolis Royal Historic Gardens occupy a site of exceptional beauty, overlooking the wetlands and meadows of a tidal river valley. More than a mile of trails meander through five theme gardens that reflect the history of the area: the Acadian Garden, encompassing a historic log house and potager (kitchen garden) and demonstrating the seventeenth-century planting practices of the area's first settlers; a Governor's Garden, in the Georgian style of the 1740s; a Victorian Garden, with ornate, nineteenth-century style flower beds; a Rose Maze planted with 1,600 bushes tracing rose culture from Elizabethan times to the present; and a Garden of the Future, demonstrating innovations in horticultural techniques. Additional plantings include a winter garden, spring garden, rock garden, perennial garden, knot garden, an evergreen collection, and a pine forest. A fountain constructed of rocks gathered from the area traces Nova Scotia's geological history from the Triassic through the Early Carboniferous ages.

The area features a number of restorations that convey its early history and settlement, which, surprisingly, predates that of Jamestown. Among these, in the salt marshes next to the gardens, is a reconstruction of the early Acadians' ingenious method of building dykes, the first such system in North America. Owned and operated by the Annapolis Royal Historic Gardens Society, the grounds were opened to the public in 1981.

Pink hostas and yellow daylilies dab an Annapolis pond setting with color.

HALIFAX PUBLIC GARDENS
Halifax

Flower carpets, serpentine and scroll beds, cast-iron fountains, and a gingerbread bandstand acknowledge Halifax Public Gardens' debt to the Victorian era. Indeed the bandstand and one of the facility's fountains were erected in honor of Queen Victoria's Golden and Diamond jubilees, respectively. In fact, these gardens could be described collectively as one of the most complete examples extant in North America of what some would describe as the excessive ornateness of nineteenth-century gardening. Classical stone bridges (ca. 1911), a sundial, statuary, rockeries, perennial borders, and a tropical bed planted out each summer with palms, agaves, dracaenas, aloes, and birds of paradise complete the Victorian-bountiful impression.

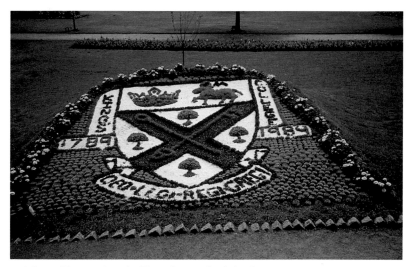

Halifax Public Gardens' bedding designs hark back to Victorian practices.

These remarkable gardens have been a City of Halifax landmark since 1830, when a group of citizens formed the Nova Scotia Horticultural Society and built a garden to demonstrate "the cultivation of choice fruit trees, vegetables, rare plants and flowers." This and two adjoining civic gardens were incorporated into a unified plan, drawn up by Richard Power in 1874, that completed the grounds as they exist today. Among the many memorable features are a stone grotto, beds of showy dahlias, and distinctive specimen trees, numbering among them many weeping and flowering varieties. The gardens are maintained, along with 200 other community parks and forested areas, by the Parks and Grounds Division of the Engineering and Works Department of the City of Halifax.

ONTARIO

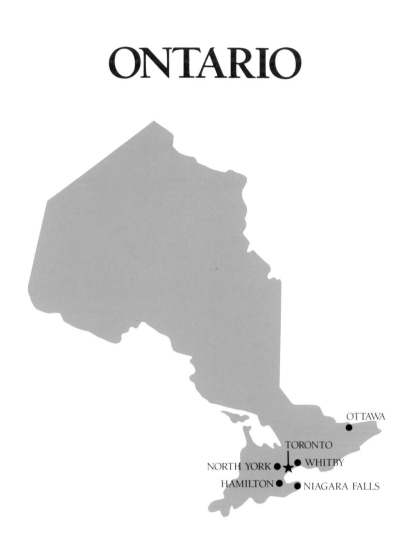

OTTAWA

TORONTO

NORTH YORK ● ● WHITBY

HAMILTON ● ● NIAGARA FALLS

DUNDURN CASTLE AND WHITEHERN
Hamilton

Two restorations that are examples of gracious nineteenth-century living are within blocks of each other in Hamilton, Ontario. Dundurn Castle, a 35-room Italianate-style villa and National Historic Site, was built in 1832 for Sir Allan Napier MacNab, Upper Canada's pre-Confederation Prime Minister. The site was reconstructed in 1967 to appear as it did in 1855 when MacNab was at the peak of his political career. Its rooms are furnished with authentic period pieces and its gardens are graced with century-old trees and shrubs and appropriate latter-day beds of annuals and perennials.

Whitehern was built in 1852 for the McQuesten family whose most well-known member, T. B. McQuesten, was one of the principal developers of the Royal Botanical Gardens (see p. 118). The mansion remained in the possession of the family until it was bequeathed to the people of Hamilton in 1968. Its one acre of terraced gardens and Victorian urn plantings, charmingly evocative of a more romantic age, evolved over three McQuesten generations. The grounds are maintained today with as many of the original plant choices in place as possible. The sunken area at the rear of the house was designed in the early 1930s by H. B. Dunnington-Grubb, the architect who laid out Gage Park (see p. 117). Indeed, the McQuestens were instrumental in creating Hamilton's system of city parks, one of Canada's finest. Dundurn Castle and Whitehern are administered by the City of Hamilton's Department of Culture and Recreation.

Dundurn Castle looms majestically over its Centennial Rose Garden.

Gage Park is the site of a chrysanthemum extravaganza every fall.

GAGE PARK
Hamilton

During the first two weeks of November every year, Gage Park is a riot of chrysanthemums. Boasting 60,000 blooms representing 125 varieties, the spectacular Mum Show draws visitors from far and wide. Otherwise, this 75-acre green oasis, designed by landscape architect H. B. Dunnington-Grubb and opened to the public in 1924, encompasses a rose garden with over 5,000 bushes, two bowling greens, and a spacious conservatory with an extensive collection of tropicals. At chrysanthemum time, this enclosed environment is transformed into a wonderland of cascading, hanging, and upright forms of the brightly colored blooms. Children's attractions at the facility include a museum and a play area with a wading pool. The Corporation of the City of Hamilton founded the park and continues to oversee its operation and maintenance.

ROYAL BOTANICAL GARDENS
Hamilton

Encompassing almost 2,700 acres of gardens and conservation areas, the Royal Botanical Gardens is one of the great research facilities in North America, offering enormous collections of plants and beautiful display gardens for the enjoyment of the public. The concept of a botanical garden for southern Ontario dates back to the late 1920s. Land on what was once a quarry known as Kerr's Gravel Pits was acquired in 1929, and— fortuitously providing work for scores of the unemployed during the Great Depression—the monumental task of renovating the quarry was undertaken. The transformation was completed in 1930, and a Royal Charter in 1941 officially designated this site and others as the Royal Botanical Gardens, linking them with the celebrated institutions of Kew, Edinburgh, and Sydney, as well as others in Trinidad, Jamaica, Sri Lanka, and India.

A cascade of spring tulips fronts the Royal Botanical Gardens teahouse.

Today, the facility oversees a number of attractive habitats, including woodlands, meadows, shallow lake, marsh, agricultural land, and ornamental displays. Scattered throughout the Hamilton area, the latter include: the Laking Garden, with one of the world's largest and most magnificent displays of irises, as well as hundreds of kinds of peonies in spring and perennials in summer; Hendrie Park, exhibiting thousands of roses, a trial garden, a collection of clematis, a medicinal garden, and a scented garden;

a 40-acre arboretum proffering native trees, flowering trees of all kinds, and an outstanding lilac collection; the Rock Garden, with its great drifts of tulips in spring and annuals, begonias, and impatiens in summer. The Royal Botanical Gardens Centre shelters permanent indoor collections and seasonal displays.

The institution schedules a rich diversity of courses, exhibitions, lectures, and concerts, and its comprehensive library is available for use by the public. The Children's Garden, a 15-acre tract, exposes young people to the delights of gardening.

The RBG is generously funded by the Ontario Ministry of Culture and Communications, and the Regional Municipalities of Hamilton-Wentworth and Halton. Additional financial support is derived from foundations, organizations, and membership.

Daffodils populate Queen Victoria Park in spring.

NIAGARA PARKS
Niagara Falls

In the vicinity of the Canadian Horseshoe Falls, The Niagara Parks Commission owns and maintains three colorful display gardens, each with its own special features:

At 200-acre Queen Victoria Park, elegant formal landscaping stands out boldly against the spectacular backdrop of the mighty falls in the distance. Plantings of bulbs (500,000 daffodils, the largest such display in North America), annuals (40,000), perennials, coleus, dahlias, lantana standards, rosebushes, and a rock garden provide spectacular color from season to season. On the grounds, a quarter mile south of the falls, is a conservatory encompassing tropical and seasonal display houses. The latter offers shows of poinsettias, cyclamen, and Christmas cacti (December 8–January 31), Easter lilies, bulbs, and cinerarias (February 1–May 31), caladiums and hydrangeas (June 7–September 6), Reiger begonias (September 7–October 7), and chrysanthemums and amaryllis (October 8–December 7).

Also within the park is the Oakes Garden Theatre, a Greco-Roman–style outdoor amphitheater with terraced and rock gardens, topiaries, and lily ponds.

A Canadian landmark seven miles north of the falls, the Floral Clock and Lilac Garden is famed for its giant working timepiece composed of 25,000 flowering plants. At peak bloom in late May at the site are 1,500 lilac bushes representing 250 varieties.

Coleus topped by lantana at Niagara Parks School of Horticulture.

NIAGARA PARKS COMMISSION SCHOOL OF HORTICULTURE
Niagara Falls

In the early 1900s, as immigration of skilled gardeners from Europe began to ebb, the Niagara Parks Commission recognized the need to establish a school of horticulture to supply trained personnel for the cultivation of its gardens. But it was not until 1936 that enrollment began and 100 acres of a narrow band of land between the Whirlpool and the Niagara Glen (five miles north of the Horseshoe Falls) became the site of a school for apprentices "to learn the art, trade or mystery of a gardener." Today, the commission supervises a system of parks stretching from Lake Erie to Lake Ontario comprising 2,800 acres, and the students are responsible for the maintenance and development of the facility's 100-acre campus.

Encompassing perennial borders, a vegetable garden, an annual garden, a woodland garden, a nature trail, an aviary, a rock garden, flowering trees and shrubs, formal-design flower beds, and herb and rose gardens, the horticultural installations exemplify the spectacular year-round color and degree of perfection characteristic of all of Canada's Niagara Falls gardens. From early spring to late fall, the school's flowering collections schedule a nonstop show of color. These include: flowering bulbs (April 15–May 30); Japanese cherry trees (May 10–May 20); lilacs (May 15–June 5); rhododendrons (May 25–June 10); irises (May 24–June 30); peonies (June 10–June 20); roses (June 15–September 30); chrysanthemums (September 15–first frost); and the rock garden and perennial borders (April 15–October 15).

Edwards Gardens counts lilacs among its collections of flowering shrubs.

EDWARDS GARDENS AND THE CIVIC GARDEN CENTRE
North York

Providing a 35-acre garden park for walking, jogging, or just plain relaxing amid nature's finery, Edwards Gardens has been a joy to its constituency since 1956 when it first opened as a public facility. Its wide variety of settings, including rolling lawns, a stream spanned by rustic bridges, a 500-foot-long rock garden hugging the banks of Wilket Creek, lavish floral displays, and natural woodlands, entices droves of visitors throughout the seasons.

The site was originally settled in 1817 by Alexander Milne who purchased 600 acres and built three mills along the Don River. After more than a century of Milne-family ownership, the parcel passed through a series of hands, until 1944 when it was acquired by Rupert E. Edwards. Anxious to turn the property into a congenial country retreat, it was Mr. Edwards who installed the ambitious rock garden and filled 27 additional acres with curving paths, pools, a fountain and wishing well, extensive flower beds, and a nine-hole golf course, some tees of which are still evident. To ensure the preservation of his creation and avert subdivision, Mr. Edwards eventually sold the site to Metropolitan Toronto for a fraction of its true value. Today, it is operated and maintained by the Toronto Parks Department.

Continuing its tradition of impressive floral displays, Edwards boasts more than 1,000 rhododendrons and azaleas. Planted under the auspices of the Toronto Chapter of The Rhododendron Society of Canada, these are ablaze with bloom from mid-April until late June. Thousands of spring bulbs add brightness to the months of April and May, while lilacs, roses, annuals, and perennials take over during the summer. Especially intriguing and informative for children are the many kinds of wildlife that inhabit all areas of the park.

The grounds also provide a home for one of Canada's most extensive and respected gardening education facilities. The Civic Garden Centre dispenses information and inspiration through a wide array of activities, including flower shows, workshops, courses, exhibits, and lectures. Its horticultural library of more than 6,000 titles encompasses every aspect of the art of gardening. An independent nonprofit organization, the center is supported by membership dues, fund-raising projects, and donations from The Edwards Foundation and other benefactors.

CENTRAL EXPERIMENTAL FARM
Ottawa

One would hardly expect to find a working farm, complete with crops, livestock, and a dairy barn, smack in the middle of a bustling city. But the unexpected awaits in Canada's capital. A research facility of Agriculture Canada, governmental advisor to the nation's farmers, the Central Experimental Farm was the first of five such installations established across Canada in the wake of the Experimental Farm Stations Act of 1886. The fascinating and well-organized complex today offers a number of exhibits that succeed in delighting and informing all members of the family. Various breeds of beef cattle, swine, sheep, and horses may be inspected in their respective barns, after which visitors may hop aboard the Tally-Ho wagon, drawn by two Clydesdales, for a 15-minute tour of the farm.

Among the more gardening oriented attractions are the Macoun Sunken Garden, the Rock Garden, and the Ornamental Gardens. These display an abundant variety of flowers and shrubs, including lilacs, peonies, hostas,

Morden's pink lithrum dominates Central Experimental Farm's ornamental garden.

geraniums, all kinds of annuals and perennials, and new releases of Explorer roses, weigelas, forsythias, and mock oranges. A hedges garden demonstrates the best shrub and tree choices, including Douglas firs and hemlocks, for hedging in the Ottawa area. A greenhouse in the complex offers 500 varieties of tropicals, including orchids, cacti, and banana trees, and a spectacular chrysanthemum display in early November. The farm's expansive arboretum is planted with more than 2,000 woody specimens, including magnolias, rhododendrons, azaleas, crab apples, Ponderosa pines, metasequoia, and a wisteria. Among the facility's 140 buildings, devoted mostly to agricultural and horticultural research, is an astronomical observatory built in 1902. Its entrance plaza adorned with a sundial made of flower beds, the historic structure is no longer used to scan the heavens, but houses an exhibit of instruments designed to measure earthquakes, tides, and the earth's magnetic field.

CULLEN GARDENS AND MINIATURE VILLAGE
Whitby

Nursery owner Len Cullen acquired a 150-acre tract of land in 1966 that included a scenic valley of meadows and giant cedars. Inspired by the show gardens and theme attractions he had seen throughout the world, he began reworking the land into his own personal vision, one that encompassed ponds, streams, covered bridges, period buildings, topiaries, planting beds, and scenes in miniature (a village, with 150 replicas of existing buildings in southern Ontario, a lakeshore resort, and a county fair). The finished transformation opened to the public in 1980.

The artfully landscaped acreage plays host to a Christmas Festival of Lights (November–January), a winter carnival featuring ice sculptures (December–January), a Tulip Festival (April–May) with more than 100,000 blooms, a Rose Festival (June–July) with 10,000 blooms, and a Chrysanthemum Show (mid-September). Floral-carpet designs planted with thousands of annuals and a nature trail are more of the many features of interest to the gardener. A historic structure, the Lynde House, built in 1803, features animated figures in a realistic portrayal of home life in the mid-nineteenth century.

The miniature villages at Cullen Gardens host a tulip festival each spring.

QUEBEC

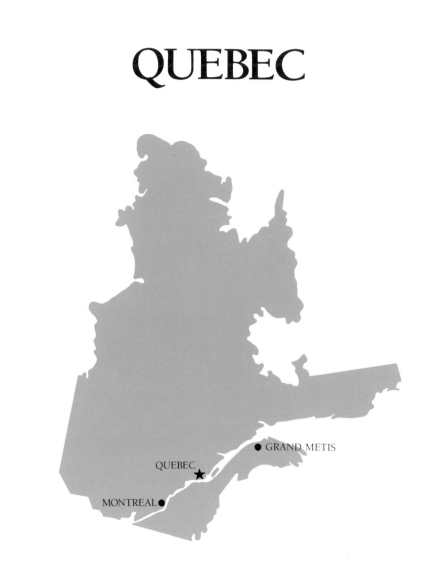

METIS GARDENS
Grand Metis

Filled with glorious bloom from spring into fall, this 45-acre garden represents the singular vision and devotion to horticulture of Elsie Neighen Reford. Having inherited a salmon-fishing camp from an uncle in 1919, Lady Reford transformed the site over a period of eight years into a luxurious villa. Gathering more than 1,500 kinds of plants from around the world, including 500 species of perennials, she continued the development of the property's gardens until her death in 1954. Her legacy of beauty was acquired in 1961 by the government of Quebec, which set about restoring the gardens to their original splendor and making them accessible to the public.

Six scenic garden settings offer lavish bloom in the form of rhododendrons, flowering shrubs and fruit trees, alpines, annuals, and Lady Reford's beloved perennials, many never seen this far north until her arrival. The emblem of the garden is the legendary blue poppy. Native to the alpine prairies of the Himalayas and in bloom throughout the month of July, the elusive flower offers one of the clearest, loveliest blues to be found in all of horticulture. Dating from 1887, the villa's main house today contains a museum and a crafts shop.

Metis Gardens' rockery, stocked with alpines, perennials, and conifers.

MONTREAL BOTANICAL GARDEN
Montreal

One of the most exciting, comprehensive, and diverse botanic gardens in all of North America, the 180-acre Montreal Botanical Garden, founded in 1931 by Brother Marie-Victorin (1885–1944), offers 26,000 species and varieties of plants in 30 specialized gardens and nine exhibition greenhouses. Originally laid out by the garden's first curator, Henry Teuscher, the grounds feature magnificent formal gardens with pools and fountains, an arboretum of rare old specimens, a marsh and bog garden and other natural habitats, an alpine garden, annual (500 species) and vegetable test gardens, and endless other collections and displays.

Among the all-encompassing institution's highlights, promising something of interest for everyone, are: the greenhouse, with permanent collections of orchids, bromeliads, gesneriads, begonias, ferns, cacti and succulents, one of the finest gatherings in the world of Japanese bonsai and the Chinese variety, penjing, and spring, fall, and Christmas seasonal installations; the rose gardens, containing 8,000 bushes; a heath garden; a perennial garden; a brook garden, displaying such flowering varieties as peonies, irises, and daylilies; medicinal and poisonous plant gardens; and a children's garden devoted to and tended entirely by young people. The seasonal festivals of spring daffodils and tulips and fall chrysanthemums are spectacular, attracting thousands of admirers every year.

Dedicated to information and education, the garden presents changing exhibits of all kinds and schedules lectures, special events, and courses. The Louis Reil Horticultural School on the premises offers a two-year training program in professional horticulture. The vast facility, made accessible by train tours, is owned and operated by the City of Montreal.

Richly hued lupines attract attention at Montreal Botanical Garden.

VISITORS' INFORMATION

KEY TO SYMBOLS

Brochures

Gift shop

Parking

Guided tours

Labels

Visitors' center

Picnic facilities

Membership

Restaurant

Courses

THE UNITED STATES

CONNECTICUT

CONNECTICUT COLLEGE ARBORETUM
New London, CT 06320
(203) 447-7700 ▇ 및 ▣

Directions	New London is located on the Connecticut coastline; from New York City, I-95 to Exit 83; follow Rte. 32 north about ¼ mi. to the campus on the left; cross the campus to the arboretum gate at Williams St.
Hours	Every day, dawn to dusk; publications available business hours at Arboretum Office, 206 New London Hall.
Admission	No fee.
Wheelchair access	Limited.
Special features	College campus; rustic lodge; outdoor theater.

BARTLETT ARBORETUM
University of Connecticut   151 Brookdale Road   Stamford, CT 06903
(203) 322-6971 ▇ **P** 및 **GT** ⑦ ▣ ↵

Directions	Located approximately 6 mi. north of Stamford; from New York City, take Merritt Pkwy. (Rte. 15) to Exit 35 north; High Ridge Rd. (Rte. 137) 1 mi. to Brookdale Rd., turn left and continue to entrance on the right.
Hours	Grounds, every day 8:30 A.M. to sunset; administration building (visitor center) and library, weekdays 8:30 A.M. to 4 P.M.; for guided tours, call in advance for a reservation.
Admission	No fee.
Wheelchair access	None.
Special features	Horticultural library; herbarium; outdoor classroom.

DELAWARE

MT. CUBA CENTER FOR THE STUDY OF PIEDMONT FLORA
P.O. Box 3570   Greenville, DE 19807
(302) 239-4244 ⬛ P ⬦ GT

Directions	Located about 6 mi. northeast of Wilmington.
Hours	Open to interested groups of 10 to 15 by advance reservation only; call the above number.
Admission	No fee.
Wheelchair access	None.

THE GEORGE READ II HOUSE AND GARDEN
42 The Strand   New Castle, DE 19720
(302) 322-8411 ⬛ ⬛ GT

Directions	The historic district of New Castle is located 7 mi. south of Wilmington, on the shores of the Delaware River.
Hours	March 1 to December 31, Tuesday through Saturday 10 A.M. to 4 P.M.; Sunday noon to 4 P.M.; January and February, weekends only; closed major holidays.
Admission	Combination fee charged for house and garden, or single fee for garden alone; group tours and guided tours by advance reservation; walking tours of New Castle available.
Wheelchair access	Throughout.
Special features	Historic restoration.

THE HOMESTEAD
Rehoboth Art League, Inc.   12 Dodds Lane   Henlopen Acres   Rehoboth Beach, DE 19971
(302) 227-8408 ⬛ P ⬦ GT

Directions	Located at the intersection of Dodds Lane and Rolling Rd. in Rehoboth Beach, a seaside community on the Atlantic coast in southern Delaware.
Hours	Mid-May to mid-October, Monday through Saturday 10 A.M. to 4 P.M., Sunday noon to 4 P.M.
Admission	No fee.
Wheelchair access	Throughout.
Special features	Historic restoration; art gallery.

ELEUTHERIAN MILLS
Hagley Museum and Library   P.O. Box 3630   Route 141   Wilmington, DE 19807
(302) 658-2400   ∎P ⌂ ⏚ ✕ ⛊ GT ⑦

Directions	Located 45 mins. from Philadelphia, on Rte. 141; from I-95, take Exit 7 (Delaware Ave.) to Rte. 52 north, to Rte. 100 north, to Rte. 141 north; or take Exit 8 (Rte. 202 north) to Rte. 141 south, and follow signs to Hagley.
Hours	April through December, every day 9:30 A.M. to 4:30 P.M.; January though March, weekends 9:30 A.M. to 4:30 P.M.; guided tour given at 1:30 P.M. on weekdays, January through March; call for reservations.
Admission	Fee charged; no fee for children age 5 and under; special family rate.
Wheelchair access	Throughout.
Special features	Historic restoration; museum; craft and industrial demonstrations.

NEMOURS MANSION AND GARDENS
P.O. Box 109   Rockland Road   Wilmington, DE 19899
(302) 651-6912   ∎P GT ⑦

Directions	Located about 4 mi. north of Wilmington; I-95 to U.S. 202 north; left at Rte. 141; left at Rockland Rd.
Hours	All visits by guided tours: May through November, Tuesday through Saturday 9 and 11 A.M., 1 and 3 P.M.; Sunday 11 A.M., 1 and 3 P.M.; advance reservations recommended for individuals and required for groups; call above number, Monday through Friday 8:30 A.M. to 4:30 P.M.; all visitors must be at least 16 years of age, and must arrive at reception center at least 15 min. prior to tour.
Admission	Fee charged.
Wheelchair access	None (many stairways to negotiate).
Special features	Estate restoration.

ROCKWOOD MUSEUM
610 Shipley Road   Wilmington, DE 19809
(302) 571-7776 🚪P⚓👥GT 📷

Directions	Located north of downtown Wilmington; I-95 to Exit 9 (Marsh Rd.); south on Marsh Rd.; right on Washington St.; right on Shipley Rd.
Hours	Tuesday through Saturday 11 A.M. to 4 P.M.; guided tours conducted 11 A.M. to 3 P.M.; closed major holidays; group tours of 10 or more by advance reservation; reference library, Tuesday through Friday 11 A.M. to 4 P.M.
Admission	Fee charged for house and garden tours; no fee for children age 4 and under; no fee for self-guided tour of the grounds.
Wheelchair access	Limited.
Special features	Historic restoration.

WINTERTHUR MUSEUM AND GARDENS
Winterthur, DE 19735
(302) 654-1548 🚪P⚓✕👥GT ⑦ 📖

Directions	Located 35 mi. south of Philadelphia and 5 mi. northwest of Wilmington, on Rte. 52.
Hours	Tuesday through Saturday 10 A.M. to 4 P.M.; Sunday noon to 4 P.M.; closed Thanksgiving, New Year's Day, and December 24 and 25; tram tours with guides scheduled throughout the day.
Admission	Fee charged.
Wheelchair access	Throughout.
Special features	Estate restoration.

MAINE

WILD GARDENS OF ACADIA
Acadia National Park   Sieur de Monts Spring   Bar Harbor, ME 04609
(207) 288-3338 ▉P ⛲

Directions	Located on the Maine coast, in Acadia National Park, just outside Bar Harbor on Mt. Desert Island.
Hours	Every day, May through October, 8 A.M. to 8 P.M.
Admission	No fee.
Wheelchair access	Throughout.

MERRYSPRING
P.O. Box 893   Camden, ME 04843
(207) 236-8831 ▉P ⛲ ▥ ♫

Directions	Camden is located along the Maine coast on U.S. 1; from Camden, take U.S. 1 south; right on Conway Rd., continue to the road's end.
Hours	Every day, dawn to dusk.
Admission	No fee.
Wheelchair access	Throughout.

DEERING OAKS ROSE CIRCLE
Department of Parks and Public Works   55 Portland Street   Portland, ME 04101
(207) 874-8871 ▉P ⛲ ⚓ ✗

Directions	Located in Deering Oaks Park, along Park Ave.
Hours	Every day, dawn to 10 P.M.; group tours by advance reservation.
Admission	No fee.
Wheelchair access	Throughout.

HAMILTON HOUSE
Vaughan's Lane   South Berwick, ME 03908
(207) 384-5269 ▊**P** ▣

Directions	Located about 2 mi. south of the center of South Berwick, near the New Hampshire border; I-95 to Rte. 236 north; after the junction with Rte. 91, take first left onto Brattle St.; take second right onto Vaughan's Lane.
Hours	June 1 to October 15, Tuesday, Thursday, Saturday, and Sunday noon to 5 P.M.
Admission	Fee charged.
Wheelchair access	Most areas.
Special features	Historic restoration; picnic facilities at nearby Vaughan Woods Memorial State Park.

MASSACHUSETTS

SEDGWICK GARDENS AT LONG HILL
572 Essex Street   Beverly, MA 01915
(508) 921-1944   ▇P♀⚲GT▣

Directions	Located about 30 mi. northeast of downtown Boston; Rte. 128 to Exit 18; north on Rte. 22 (Essex St.) 1 mi. (bearing left at fork) to brick gateposts and sign on left; proceed to parking area.
Hours	Gardens, every day 8 A.M. to dusk; house, by appointment only; guided tours by appointment.
Admission	Fee charged; no fee for children age 14 and under.
Wheelchair access	Throughout.
Special features	Estate restoration; annual plant sale; horticultural lectures.

ISABELLA STEWART GARDNER MUSEUM
280 The Fenway   Boston, MA 02115
Mailing address: 2 Palace Road   Boston, MA 02115
(617) 566-1401   ▇✕♙▣

Directions	Massachusetts Tpke. to Exit 22; south on Huntington Ave. (Rte. 9); right on Longwood Ave.; right on Palace Rd.; right on The Fenway.
Hours	September through June, Tuesday noon to 6:30 P.M., Wednesday through Sunday noon to 5 P.M.; July through August, Tuesday through Sunday noon to 5 P.M.; the cafe, Tuesday noon to 6:30 P.M., Wednesday through Sunday noon to 4:30 P.M.; July through August, Tuesday through Sunday noon to 4:30 P.M.
Admission	Fee charged; no fee on Wednesday.
Wheelchair access	Throughout.
Special features	Historic restoration; art galleries.

LONGFELLOW NATIONAL HISTORIC SITE
105 Brattle Street   Cambridge, MA 02138
(617) 566-1689   ▇GT

Directions	Located in historic Cambridge; follow Brattle St. west from Harvard Square; house is located six blocks up the street on the right; nearby restorations include the Vassall and Brattle Houses.
Hours	Every day 9 A.M. to 5 P.M. except Thanksgiving, New Year's Day, and Christmas Day.
Admission	No fee for garden; small fee for house.
Wheelchair access	Gardens, throughout; house by advance notice.
Special features	Historic restoration.

MOUNT AUBURN CEMETERY
580 Mount Auburn Street   Cambridge, MA 02138
(617) 547-7105 ▊P ⛾ GT ◱

Directions	Located on Rte. 16 at the Cambridge-Watertown boundary line.
Hours	Every day 8 A.M. to 5 P.M.; during daylight saving time, closing is at 7 P.M.; guided tours available by advance reservation; maps and other publications available in the office during business hours.
Admission	No fee; fee charged for guided tours.
Wheelchair access	Throughout.
Special features	60-ft. tower with view of Boston; historic Victorian monuments, temples and sculptures; two historic churches.

GARDEN IN THE WOODS
Hemenway Road   Framingham, MA 01701
(508) 877-6574 ▊P ⛾ ⅲ GT ⑦ ◱ ◿

Directions	Located 40 mins. from Boston and Worcester; Rte. 128 to Rte. 20 (west); 8 mi. on Rte. 20 to Raymond Rd. (2nd left after traffic lights in South Sudbury); 1.3 mi. to Hemenway Rd.
Hours	April 15 to October 31, Tuesday through Sunday 9 A.M. to 4 P.M.; closed Monday; guided tours by advance reservation; informal walks with a guide, Tuesday and Friday 10 A.M.
Admission	Fee charged; no fee for children age 4 and under.
Wheelchair access	Limited.
Special features	Horticultural and botanical library; New England Wild Flower Society publications.

THE ARNOLD ARBORETUM OF HARVARD UNIVERSITY
125 Arborway   Jamaica Plain, MA 02130-2795
(617) 524-1718 ▊P ⛾ ⅲ GT ⑦ ◱

Directions	The main gate is located 100 yds. south of the junction of Rte. 1 south and Rte. 203 (Arborway); from US 95, exit Rte. 1 and continue to junction of Rtes. 1 and 203. Accessible from Boston by public transportation; call for directions.
Hours	Grounds open every day of the year from dawn to dusk; Hunnewell Visitor Center open weekdays (except holidays) 9 A.M. to 4 P.M., weekends 10 A.M. to 4 P.M.; Dana Greenhouses, Wednesday 1:30 to 4 P.M.
Admission	No fee.
Wheelchair access	Along paved walkways throughout the grounds.

CODMAN HOUSE, THE GRANGE
Codman Road   Lincoln, MA 01773
(617) 259-8843 **■ P GT** ▣

Directions	Lincoln is located about 20 mi. west of Boston; Rte. 2 west to Rte. 126 (Concord Rd.) south; left on Codman Rd.
Hours	June 1 to October 15, Wednesday through Sunday; guided tours at noon, 1, 2, 3, and 4 P.M.
Admission	Gardens, no fee; house, fee charged.
Wheelchair access	Gardens, throughout; house, none.
Special features	Historic restoration; carriage house.

JEREMIAH LEE MANSION
161 Washington Street   P.O. Box 1048   Marblehead, MA 01945
(617) 631-1069 **■ GT**

Directions	Located about 20 mi. north of Boston's city center; Rte. 1A to Rte. 129 to Marblehead.
Hours	Gardens, every day, dawn to dusk; closed mid-October to mid-May; group tours of the mansion by advance reservation.
Admission	No fee.
Wheelchair access	Limited.
Special features	Historic restoration.

BOTANIC GARDEN OF SMITH COLLEGE
Smith College   Northampton, MA 01063
(413) 584-2700 **■ P ⛲ GT**

Directions	Located 1 mi. west of the center of Northampton, near the intersection of College Lane and Elm St. (Rte. 9); I-91 to exit 19; continue on Rte. 9 north through Northampton; left on College Lane; one block to Lyman Plant House.
Hours	Grounds, every day at all times; greenhouse, every day 8 A.M. to 4 P.M.; group tours by advance reservation.
Admission	No fee.
Wheelchair access	Throughout.
Special features	College campus.

ROPES MANSION
318 Essex Street   Salem, MA 01970
(508) 744-3390 ∎ **GT**

Directions	Salem is located approximately 20 mi. northeast of Boston; the mansion is situated in the city's center.
Hours	Garden, spring through fall, Monday through Saturday 8 A.M. to 4 P.M.; mansion, June through October, Tuesday through Saturday 10 A.M. to 4 P.M., Sunday 1 to 5 P.M., with tours scheduled every half hour.
Admission	No fee for garden; fee charged for mansion.
Wheelchair access	Garden is accessible, mansion is not.
Special features	Historic restoration.

HERITAGE PLANTATION OF SANDWICH
Grove and Pine Streets   Sandwich, MA 02563
(508) 888-3300 ∎ **P** ♔ ⚿ 🏛 **GT**

Directions	Located 1 mi. from the center of Sandwich, on the northwest end of Cape Cod; from Sagamore Bridge, exit to Rte. 6A; take Rte. 130 to Pine St. and the plantation.
Hours	Mid-May through late October, every day 10 A.M. to 5 P.M.
Admission	Fee charged; no fee for children age 5 and under.
Wheelchair access	Throughout.
Special features	Estate restoration; museum galleries with objects of interest to children.

BERKSHIRE GARDEN CENTER
Stockbridge, MA 01262
(413) 298-3926 ∎ **P** ♔ ⚿ 🏛 **GT** ⊘ 📧 ⚲

Directions	Located on both sides of Rte. 102, just past the intersections of Rtes. 102 and 183 and 2 mi. west of the center of Stockbridge; from the Massachusetts Tpke., take Exit 2 (Rte. 102) west.
Hours	Grounds, mid-May to mid-October, every day 10 A.M. to 5 P.M.; greenhouses and offices open year-round; group tours by advance reservation.
Admission	Fee charged May to October.
Wheelchair access	Most areas.
Special features	Restored farmhouses; herb products shop; horticultural library.

NAUMKEAG
Prospect Hill Road   P.O. Box 792   Stockbridge, MA 01262
(413) 298-3239 ∎ P ⊥ GT ▣

Directions	From intersection of Rtes. 7 and 102 at the Red Lion Inn in Stockbridge center, take Pine St. north; bear left on Prospect Hill Rd. ½ mi.; entrance on left.
Hours	Gardens, every day 10 A.M. to 5 P.M.; house, late June through Labor Day, Tuesday through Sunday and Monday holidays; Memorial Day weekend to late June and Labor Day to Columbus Day, Saturday, Sunday, and Monday holidays; 10 A.M. to 4:15 P.M. on all days open.
Admission	Separate fees charged for house and garden, or combination fee for both; no fees for children age 5 and under; group rate by advance reservation.
Wheelchair access	Most areas.
Special features	Estate restoration.

OLD STURBRIDGE VILLAGE
1 Old Sturbridge Village Road   Sturbridge, MA 01566
(508) 347-3362 ∎ P ⟐ ⊥ ✗ 🛏 ⊘

Directions	Located 1 hr. from Boston and Hartford, 3½ hrs. from New York City; on Rte. 20 west, near Exit 9 of the Massachusetts Tpke. (I-90) and Exit 2 of I-84.
Hours	May through October, every day 9 A.M. to 5 P.M.; November through April, Tuesday through Sunday 10 A.M. to 4 P.M.; exceptions to Monday closings: Christmas week, Martin Luther King's birthday, Washington's birthday, 3rd Monday in April (Massachusetts Patriots Day).
Admission	Fee charged; no fee for children age 5 and under.
Wheelchair access	Throughout.
Special features	Historic restoration; crafts demonstrations; from April through October, all gardens are staffed by costumed workers who will discuss what they are doing and answer questions.

LYMAN ESTATE, THE VALE
185 Lyman Street   Waltham, MA 02154
(617) 893-7232 (rental of facilities, group tours)
(617) 891-7095 (greenhouse) 🚻 **GT** ⊠

Directions	Waltham is located 10 mi. northwest of Boston; take U.S. 20 (Main St.); turn right on Lyman St.; entrance is at the corner of Lyman and Beaver Sts.
Hours	Grounds, all times; greenhouses and plant sales, Monday through Saturday 9 A.M. to 3 P.M.; group tours by advance reservation; house open to groups by appointment.
Admission	Fee charged.
Wheelchair access	Limited.
Special features	Historic restoration.

STANLEY PARK
400 Western Avenue   P.O. Box 1191   Westfield, MA 01086
(413) 568-9312 **P**

Directions	Westfield is located 10 mi. west of Springfield; Stanley Park is located in southwest Westfield, at the intersection of Western and Kensington Aves.
Hours	Mid-May to mid-October, every day 8 A.M. to dusk.
Admission	No fee.
Wheelchair access	Limited.
Special features	Recreational facilities; carillon tower; covered bridge.

THE CASE ESTATES
135 Wellesley Street   Weston, MA 02193

Mailing address: The Arnold Arboretum of Harvard University   125 Arborway Jamaica Plain, MA 02130-2795
(617) 524-1718 **P GT** ⊠

Directions	Located about 10 mi. west of Boston and 1 mi. from the Weston town center; from the Massachusetts Tpke. (Rte. 90), take exit for Rte. 30/Weston; west on Rte. 30 for 2.5 mi.; right onto Wellesley St.; entrance is 1 mi. further on the left.
Hours	Every day 9 A.M. to dusk; group tours by advance reservation.
Admission	No fee.
Wheelchair access	Throughout.

NEW HAMPSHIRE

SAINT-GAUDENS NATIONAL HISTORIC SITE
RR #2 Box 73   Cornish, NH 03745-9704
(603) 675-2175 **⬛P⬥♿ GT**

Directions	Located just off State Rte. 12A, 9 mi. north of Claremont in western New Hampshire; I-91, Exit 8 to Rte. 131 east; left onto Rte. 12A.
Hours	Memorial Day through October 31, grounds, every day 8 A.M. to dusk; buildings, 8:30 A.M. to 4:30 P.M.
Admission	Fee charged; no fee for children age 16 and under.
Wheelchair access	Throughout.
Special features	Historic restoration; exhibit galleries.

RHODODENDRON STATE PARK
Fitzwilliam, NH

Mailing address: Division of Parks and Recreation   State of New Hampshire
P.O. Box 856   Concord, NH 03301
(603) 271-3254 **⬛P**

Directions	The park is located a little over 2 mi. west of Fitzwilliam and 20 mi. east of Brattleboro, at the junction of Rtes. 12 and 119, on the southwest tip of New Hampshire.
Hours	Every day, dawn to dusk.
Admission	Fee charged late May to September 1; no fee other times.
Wheelchair access	Limited.
Special features	Historic restoration.

FULLER GARDENS
10 Willow Avenue   North Hampton, NH 03862
(603) 964-5414 **⬛P**

Directions	Located on Willow Ave., 200 yds. north of the junction of Rtes. 101-D and 1-A.
Hours	Every day 10 A.M. to 6 P.M., early May through mid-October.
Admission	Fee charged.
Wheelchair access	Throughout.
Special features	Estate restoration.

MOFFATT-LADD HOUSE AND GARDEN
154 Market Street   Portsmouth, NH 03801
(603) 436-8221 ▣ ▽ ⅲ **GT**

Directions	From Boston, I-95 north to Exit 7 east (Market St.); continue on Market St. to No. 154 (on the right, just past the intersection of Deer St.); for parking, continue on Market; turn right on Hanover; turn left into parking garage.
Hours	June 15 to October 15, Monday through Saturday 10 A.M. to 4 P.M., Sunday 2 to 5 P.M.
Admission	Fee charged.
Wheelchair access	None.
Special features	Historic restoration.

STRAWBERY BANKE
P.O. Box 300   Portsmouth, NH 03801
(603) 433-1100 ▣ **P** ⚓ ✕ ⅲ **GT** 🅼

Directions	Portsmouth is located 1 hr. north of Boston and 1 hr. south of Portland, ME; take I-95 to Exit 7 (Market St.); continue to downtown Portsmouth; museum entrance is on Marcy St., opposite Prescott Park and the waterfront.
Hours	Every day, May 1 through October 31, 10 A.M. to 5 P.M.; reopens evenings of the first two weekends in December for Candlelight Stroll.
Admission	Fee charged; no fee for children age 5 and under.
Wheelchair access	Grounds, throughout; buildings, limited.
Special features	Historic restoration; crafts demonstrations.

NEW JERSEY

LEAMING'S RUN GARDENS AND COLONIAL FARM
1845 Rte. 9 North   Cape May Court House, NJ 08210
(609) 465-5871 **⬛ P ⬛ ⬛ GT**

Directions	Located in New Jersey's southernmost peninsula, near Swainton, about 18 mi. north of the town of Cape May; Garden State Pkwy. to Exit 13 north (Rte. 9); proceed 1 mi. to No. 1845.
Hours	May 15 to October 20, every day 9:30 A.M. to 5 P.M.; Cooperage (gift shop), May 15 to Christmas, every day 10 A.M. to 5 P.M.
Admission	Fee charged; no fee for children age 5 and under.
Wheelchair access	Throughout.
Special features	Historic restoration demonstrating early farm life.

WILLOWWOOD ARBORETUM
Chester, NJ

Mailing address: Morris County Park Commission   P.O. Box 1295   Morristown, NJ 07962-1295
(201) 326-7600 **⬛ P ⬛ GT ⬛**

Directions	Chester is located about 40 mi. west of New York City; I-287 north, take Exit 18B; I-287 south, take Exit 18; proceed on Rte. 206 north about 4 mi. to Rte. 512 (Pottersville Rd.); turn left and follow posted signs to site.
Hours	Grounds, every day 8 A.M. to dusk; closed Thanksgiving, New Year's, and Christmas days; group tours by advance reservation.
Admission	No fee.
Wheelchair access	Limited.
Special features	Historic restoration; children's garden.

LEONARD J. BUCK GARDEN
Somerset County Park Commission   Horticulture Department   RD 2   Layton Road
Far Hills, NJ 07931
(908) 234-2677   **⊟P ⊈GT**

Directions	I-287 to Bedminster Exit 18B; US 202 north through Bedminster and Far Hills; right onto Liberty Corner/Far Hills Rd; continue about 1 mi.; take first right onto Layton Rd.; garden is ahead 100 yds., on the left.
Hours	Monday to Saturday 10 A.M. to 4 P.M. year round; Sundays in winter noon to 4 P.M., in summer noon to 5 P.M.; group tours by advance reservation.
Admission	No fee.
Wheelchair access	Limited.

FRELINGHUYSEN ARBORETUM
53 East Hanover Avenue   P.O. Box 1295   Morristown, NJ 07962-1295
(201) 326-7600   **⊟P ⊈GT ⦿ ▣ ⬋**

Directions	Morristown is located about 30 mi. west of New York City; I-287 north, take Exit 32B; I-287 south, take Exit 32; turn right at Ridgedale Ave.; turn right at East Hanover Ave.; entrance to arboretum is ¼ mi. up on the right.
Hours	Grounds, every day 8 A.M. to dusk; education center, every day 9 A.M. to 4:30 P.M.; closed Thanksgiving, New Year's, and Christmas days; call above number for house hours; group tours by advance reservation.
Admission	No fee.
Wheelchair access	Throughout.
Special features	Estate restoration; education center.

SKYLANDS
New Jersey State Botanical Garden   Ringwood State Park   Box 302
Ringwood, NJ 07456
(201) 962-9543   **⊟P ⊈ ⋔GT ⦿ ▣ ⬋**

Directions	Ringwood is located in northern New Jersey along the New York State border, 40 mi. from New York City; New York State Thruway (I-87) to Rte. 17 north to Sterling Mine Rd.; left at Shepard Lake Rd.
Hours	Every day, dawn to dusk.
Admission	Gardens, no fee; fee charged for mansion, which is temporarily closed for restoration; call for reopening date.
Wheelchair access	Limited.
Special features	Estate restoration.

CORA HARTSHORN ARBORETUM AND BIRD SANCTUARY
324 Forest Drive South   Short Hills, NJ 07078
(201) 376-3587 **P GT**

Directions	Located about 20 mi. west of New York City; I-78 to Morris & Essex Tpke. (Rte. 124); turn right (north) at Forest Dr.; proceed to No. 324.
Hours	Arboretum, every day, dawn to dusk; Stone House (visitor center), Tuesday through Thursday 2:30 to 4:30 P.M., Saturday 9:30 to 11:30 A.M., Sunday (October and May only) 3 to 5 P.M.
Admission	No fee.
Wheelchair access	Limited.
Special features	Stone House, containing a museum, library, nature exhibits, meeting rooms, and educational programs for preschool and school-age children, as well as adults.

RUDOLF W. VAN DER GOOT ROSE GARDEN OF COLONIAL PARK
RD 1 Mettler's Road   Somerset, NJ 08873

Mailing address: Somerset County Park Commission   Horticulture Department
RD 2 Layton Road   Far Hills, NJ 07931
(908) 234-2677 **P GT**

Directions	I-287 to Exit 7 at Weston Canal Rd.; proceed south on Canal Rd.; do not cross Weston Causeway, but turn left and continue along Canal until road turns left onto Weston Rd.; first right onto Mettler's Rd.; continue into Colonial Park; rose garden is located in the section of the park on the right (west of Mettler's Rd., Parking Lot A).
Hours	Garden, Memorial Day to Labor Day, every day 10 A.M. to 8 P.M.; Labor Day to October 31, every day 10 A.M. to 4:30 P.M.; arboretum, every day, dawn to dusk; group tours by advance reservation.
Admission	No fee.
Wheelchair access	Throughout.
Special features	Arboretum; fragrance and sensory garden.

DUKE GARDENS
P.O. Box 2030   Route 206 South   Somerville, NJ 08876
(201) 722-3700 **◼P GT**

Directions	Located about 40 mi. west of New York City and 18 mi. north of Princeton, on State Rte. 206 just south of the center of Somerville.
Hours	Every day, fall through spring, noon to 4 P.M.; closed major holidays, and from the first day of June through the last day of September because of excessive heat in the greenhouses; all visits by guided tours for which reservations must be made in advance; call the number above.
Admission	Fee charged.
Wheelchair access	None.

REEVES-REED ARBORETUM
165 Hobart Avenue   Summit, NJ 07901
(201) 273-8787   **◼P ⛾ GT ⑦ 🎞 ↵**

Directions	From New York City, Garden State Pkwy. to Rte. 78 south to Rte. 24 west; after 1.7 mi., left on Hobart Ave. and left into arboretum grounds.
Hours	Grounds, every day, dawn to dusk; Wisner House (visitor center), Monday, Tuesday, and Thursday 9 A.M. to 3 P.M.
Admission	No fee.
Wheelchair access	Throughout.
Special features	Historic restoration; discovery center for children; botanical library.

PRESBY MEMORIAL IRIS GARDENS
474 Upper Mountain Avenue   Upper Montclair, NJ 07043
(201) 783-5974   **◼P ⛾ ⚓ ⋔ GT 🎞**

Directions	Located in Mountainside Park, about 1 mi. southwest of the intersection of Rtes. US 46 and NJ 3, with easy access from I-80 and the Garden State Pkwy.
Hours	Every day, dawn to dusk, late May to October.
Admission	No fee.
Wheelchair access	Throughout the gardens, but on turf; no paved paths.

NEW YORK

CLARK GARDEN
193 I.U. Willets Road   Albertson, NY 11507
(516) 621-7568   ◘P♀⚓ⅲGT⑦ⓜ↲

Directions	From New York City, Long Island Expwy. east to Exit 37; follow LIE service road east; right onto Roslyn Rd.; right onto I.U. Willets Rd.; final right into Clark Garden parking field, just before railroad crossing.
Hours	Garden, every day 10 A.M. to 4 P.M.; gift shop, Tuesday, Wednesday, Thursday, and weekends 11:30 A.M. to 3:30 P.M.; closed Monday and Friday; guided tours, Sunday at 2 P.M., otherwise by appointment.
Admission	Fee charged.
Wheelchair access	Lawn, main paths, Clark House.
Special features	Clark House (visitor center), containing a library and classrooms; children's and seniors' vegetable gardens.

BUFFALO AND ERIE COUNTY BOTANICAL GARDENS
South Park Avenue and McKinley Parkway   Buffalo, NY 14218
(716) 828-1040   ◘P♀GTⓜ

Directions	New York State Thruway to Exit 55; west on Ridge Rd.; right on South Park Ave.; gardens are at intersection of South Park Ave. and McKinley Pkwy.
Hours	Every day, including holidays, 9 A.M. to 4 P.M.
Admission	No fee (donations accepted).
Wheelchair access	Throughout.
Special features	Historic restoration; children's learning center.

SONNENBERG GARDENS
P.O. Box 663   Canandaigua, NY 14424
(716) 924-5420   ◘P✕ⅲGTⓜ

Directions	Canandaigua is located 25 mi. southeast of Rochester, at the north end of Canandaigua Lake in the heart of the New York Finger Lakes area; from the west, New York State Thruway (I-87) to Exit 44; Rte. 332 to Canandaigua; from the east, NYS Thruway to Exit 43; Rte. 21 south to Canandaigua; Sonnenberg is located on Gibson St. (Rte. 21).
Hours	Mid-May to mid-October, every day 9:30 A.M. to 5:30 P.M.; guided tours, every day at 10 A.M. and 1 and 3 P.M.
Admission	Fee charged; no fee for children age 5 and under.
Wheelchair access	Limited.
Special features	Estate restoration.

BAYARD CUTTING ARBORETUM
Montauk Highway   Great River, NY 11739
Mailing address: P.O. Box 466   Oakdale, NY 11769
(516) 581-1002 ☐ P ♿ GT ✎

Directions	From New York City: Triborough Bridge or Queensborough (59th St.) Bridge to Queens Blvd. to Grand Central Pkwy. to Northern State Pkwy. to Sagtikos State Pkwy. south to Southern State Pkwy. east to Heckscher State Pkwy. south to Montauk Hwy. (Rte. 27A); take Exit 45E to arboretum.
Hours	Wednesday through Sunday, and legal holidays, 10 A.M. to 5 P.M. in summer, 10 A.M. to 4 P.M. in winter.
Admission	Fee charged per vehicle.
Wheelchair access	Throughout.
Special features	Estate restoration; natural history museum; picnicking and recreational activities permitted at adjoining Heckscher State Park.

VANDERBILT MANSION NATIONAL HISTORIC SITE
Frederick W. Vanderbilt Garden Association, Inc.   P.O. Box 239
Hyde Park, NY 12538-0698
(914) 229-7770 ☐ P ♿ 🍴 GT ⑦ 🅼

Directions	Hyde Park is located on the east bank of the Hudson River about 80 mi. north of New York City; take Saw Mill River Pkwy. to Taconic State Pkwy. to Rte. 55 west; right onto Rte. 9 north; continue 6 mi. to the mansion on the left.
Hours	Grounds, every day, dawn to dusk; mansion, every day, April through October, Thursday through Monday, November through March, 9 A.M. to 5 P.M.; mansion closed Thanksgiving, Christmas, and New Year's days; guided tours of the gardens available during the summer months only; group tours of the mansion by advance reservation: (914) 229-9115
Admission	Fee charged for mansion; no fee for gardens.
Wheelchair access	Mansion, throughout; gardens, none.
Special features	Estate restoration.

CORNELL PLANTATIONS
One Plantations Road   Ithaca, NY 14850-2799
(607) 255-3020   ▉ ⛲ ⚓ ⛪ **GT** ⑦ 💷 🔑

Directions	Located on the Cornell University campus, at the southern tip of Lake Cayuga; from Rte. 13 in Ithaca, take Rte. 79 east for 1.2 mi.; bear left onto Rte. 366; go 1.1 mi., then left at Judd Falls Rd.; first right after stop sign (.4 mi.); follow signs.
Hours	Every day, dawn to dusk; gift shop/visitor center, weekdays 8 A.M. to 4 P.M., weekends, mid-April to December, 11 A.M. to 5 P.M.; guided tours (fee charged) by advance reservation.
Admission	No fee.
Wheelchair access	Most areas.

BAILEY ARBORETUM
Bayville Road and Feeks Lane   Lattingtown, NY 11560
(516) 676-4497   ▉ **P** ⛲

Directions	Lattingtown is located on Long Island's North Shore, about 20 mi. east of New York City; from intersection of Rte. 25A and Wolver Hollow Rd. (Brookville Police Station), follow signs to the arboretum.
Hours	Every day, mid-April to mid-November, 9 A.M. to 4 P.M.; closed Monday.
Admission	Fee charged.
Wheelchair access	Limited.
Special features	Estate restoration.

THE JOHN P. HUMES JAPANESE STROLL GARDEN
Dogwood Lane   Mill Neck, NY

Mailing address: P.O. Box 671   Locust Valley, NY 11560
(516) 676-4486   ▉ **P GT** 💷 🔑

Directions	From New York City, Long Island Expwy. (Rte. 495) to Exit 41 north (Rte. 107); continue on 107, turn right onto Wheatley Rd.; Wheatley Rd. becomes Wolver Hollow Rd.; continue to end; turn right onto Chicken Valley Rd.; continue to Dogwood Lane; turn right, and another immediate right into the parking lot.
Hours	10 A.M. to 4 P.M. Thursday, Saturday, and Sunday, April through October; general admission and tours (Thursday and Saturday at 10 A.M. and 1:30 P.M.) by appointment only.
Admission	Fee charged.
Wheelchair access	None.
Special features	Teahouse with tea-ceremony demonstrations.

INNISFREE GARDEN
Innisfree Foundation, Inc.   Millbrook, NY 12545
(914) 677-8000 ◨P⚐

Directions	Located on Tyrrel Rd., 1 mi. from Rte. 44; from South Millbrook on Rte. 44 (1½ mi.), turn left onto Tyrrel Rd.; from New York on Rte. 44, 1¼ mi. from the Taconic Pkwy. overpass, turn right onto Tyrrel Rd.
Hours	May through October, Wednesday through Friday 10 A.M. to 4 P.M.; weekends 11 A.M. to 5 P.M.; closed Monday and Tuesday, except Monday legal holidays.
Admission	Weekends, fee charged except for children age 15 and under; weekdays, no fee for all.
Wheelchair access	Throughout, with strong pusher.

INSTITUTE OF ECOSYSTEM STUDIES, MARY FLAGLER CARY ARBORETUM
Box AB   Route 44A   Millbrook, NY 12545-0129
(914) 677-5358 (weekdays)
(914) 677-5359 (weekends and evenings) ◨P⚐⚑🏠⑦▣♪

Directions	Located about 75 mi. north of New York City; Taconic Pkwy. to Rte. 44 east; continue 2 mi. and turn left onto Rte. 44A; after 1 mi., Gifford House is the second building on the left.
Hours	May through September, Monday through Saturday 9 A.M. to 6 P.M.; Sunday 1 to 6 P.M.; greenhouse closes every day at 4 P.M.; October through April, Monday through Saturday 9 A.M. to 4 P.M., Sunday 1 to 4 P.M.; guided tours by advance reservation.
Admission	No fee.
Wheelchair access	Most areas.
Special features	Estate restoration.

MOHONK MOUNTAIN HOUSE
Lake Mohonk   New Paltz, NY 12561
(914) 255-4500 or (212) 233-2244 ◨P⚐⚑✕🏠GT

Directions	Located 6 mi. west of New Paltz. New York State Thruway to Exit 18; west on Rte. 299; after crossing the Wallkill River, take first right; after ¼ mi., bear left at the fork, and continue up Mountain Rest Rd. to Mohonk Gate.
Hours	Gardens, every day 7 A.M. to dusk.
Admission	Fee charged; no fee for hotel guests; garden visitors may use hotel facilities for a fee.
Wheelchair access	Throughout the gardens in the immediate vicinity of the hotel.
Special features	Historic hotel facility, offering a complete range of games and sporting activities for adults, and supervised programs especially designed for children.

NEW YORK CITY

THE NEW YORK BOTANICAL GARDEN
Bronx, NY 10458-5126
(212) 220-8700 ▪P�✕🏛GT⑦🎟♿

Directions	Located in north-central Bronx; from Manhattan, take the Triborough Bridge and Bruckner Expwy. east to Bronx River Pkwy. north; take exit marked "Botanical Garden" to Southern (Kazimiroff) Blvd.; bear right and continue to NYBG main gate entrance. Accessible by public transportation (subway or bus); call for directions.
Hours	Grounds, every day except Monday, November through March, 8 A.M. to 6 P.M.; April through October, 8 A.M. to 7 P.M.; Enid A. Haupt Conservatory, Tuesday through Sunday 10 A.M. to 5 P.M.
Admission	Grounds, no fee; fee charged for the conservatory, except for children age 5 and under.
Wheelchair access	Throughout.
Special features	Historic restoration.

WAVE HILL
675 West 252nd Street   Bronx, NY 10471
(212) 549-3200 ▪P器GT⑦🎟♿

Directions	Located north of Manhattan, in the Riverdale section of the Bronx, at the intersection of Independence Ave. and 249th St.; Henry Hudson Pkwy. to 246-250th St. exit; continue north to 252nd St.; turn left at overpass; left again; right at 249th St. Accessible by public transportation (subway or bus); call for directions.
Hours	Every day 10 A.M. to 4:30 P.M.
Admission	No fee weekdays; fee charged weekends and holidays.
Wheelchair access	Limited.
Special features	Estate restoration; children's learning center; art galleries.

BROOKLYN BOTANIC GARDEN
1000 Washington Avenue   Brooklyn, NY 11225
(718) 622-4433 ∎ P ⛾ ✕ 🏛 GT ⑦ 🎫 ⤴

Directions	Located next to the Brooklyn Museum and Prospect Park; from Manhattan, take Brooklyn Bridge to Atlantic Ave.; turn left and proceed 1 mi. to Flatbush Ave.; turn right and proceed to Grand Army Plaza; go two thirds of the way around the traffic circle to Eastern Pkwy.; bear right onto Eastern Pkwy., and continue to Washington Ave.; turn right and continue about ⅛ mi. to parking lot (900 Washington Ave.) on the right. Accessible by public transportation (subway or bus); call for directions.
Hours	Grounds, April through September, Tuesday to Friday 8 A.M. to 6 P.M., weekends and holidays 10 A.M. to 6 P.M.; October through March, Tuesday to Friday 8 A.M. to 4:30 P.M., weekends and holidays 10 A.M. to 4:30 P.M.; closed on Monday, except for those that fall on public holidays; Steinhardt Conservatory, April through September, Tuesday through Sunday and holidays 10 A.M. to 5:30 P.M.; October through March 10 A.M. to 4 P.M.
Admission	Grounds, no fee; small fee charged for Steinhardt Conservatory at all times and Japanese Hill-and-Pond Garden on weekends and holidays.
Wheelchair access	Throughout.
Special features	Extensive horticultural library; historic restoration; restored glass palm house available for catered events.

QUEENS BOTANICAL GARDEN
43-50 Main Street   Flushing, NY 11355
(718) 886-3800 ∎ P ⛾ ⚓ 🏛 GT ⑦ 🎫 ⤴

Directions	Long Island Expwy. (Rte. 495) to Exit 23 (Main St.); continue northbound about 1 mi. to the garden. Accessible by public transportation (subway or bus); call for directions.
Hours	Every day 8 A.M. to dusk.
Admission	No fee.
Wheelchair access	Throughout.
Special features	Bird garden and bee garden, both especially entertaining and informative for children.

THE CENTRAL PARK CONSERVATORY GARDEN
Central Park Conservancy   The Arsenal   830 Fifth Avenue   New York, NY 10021
(212) 360-2766 ▣ ⚐ **GT**

Directions	Located in Manhattan's Central Park, toward its northeast corner; entrance is at Fifth Ave. and 105th St; metered parking is available along Fifth Ave. Accessible by public transportation (subway or bus); call the Central Park visitor information center at (212) 397-3165 for directions.
Hours	Every day 8 A.M. to dusk.
Admission	No fee.
Wheelchair access	Throughout the garden; enter Central Park at 106th St.; enter garden through north gate.

THE CLOISTERS
Fort Tryon Park   New York, NY 10040
(212) 923-3700 ▣ **P** ⚐ ⛨ **GT** ▣ ⛶

Directions	Located in Fort Tryon Park, at the northern tip of Manhattan, about 1 mi. north of the George Washington Bridge; take Henry Hudson Pkwy. north to the first exit after the George Washington Bridge. Accessible by public transportation (subway or bus); call for directions.
Hours	Every day, except Monday, March through October, 9:30 A.M. to 5:15 P.M.; November through February 9:30 A.M. to 4:45 P.M.; closed Thanksgiving, Christmas, and New Year's days.
Admission	No fee; donation requested.
Wheelchair access	Limited.
Special features	Medieval art collection; historic restoration.

OLD WESTBURY GARDENS
P.O. Box 430   71 Old Westbury Road   Old Westbury, NY 11568
(516) 333-0048   ⬛ P ⬦ ⬧ ⬥ GT ▣ ⬩

Directions	From New York City, Long Island Expwy. (Rte. 495) to Glen Cove Rd. (Exit 39S); follow service road eastbound 1.2 mi.; turn right onto Old Westbury Rd.; continue ¼ mi. to gardens.
Hours	Wednesday through Sunday 10 A.M. to 5 P.M., from late April through October, including Memorial Day, July 4, Labor Day, and Columbus Day.
Admission	Separate fees charged for house and gardens.
Wheelchair access	Limited.
Special features	Estate restoration.

PLANTING FIELDS ARBORETUM
Planting Fields Road   Oyster Bay, NY 11771
(516) 922-9200   ⬛ P ⬦ ⬥ GT ⦿ ▣ ⬩

Directions	Oyster Bay is located on Long Island's North Shore, about 25 mi. east of New York City; Long Island Expwy. (Rte. 495) to Exit 41 north; Rte. 106 to Rte. 25A; left (west) on 25A; right on Mill River Rd.; north to Glen Cove Rd.; left on Planting Fields Rd.; entrance is on the left.
Hours	Grounds, every day 9 A.M. to 5 P.M.; camellia house, 10 A.M. to 4 P.M.; main greenhouse, 10 A.M. to 4:30 P.M.; closed Christmas Day; Coe Hall (main house), April through September, weekdays 1 to 3:30 P.M. for 45-minute guided tours; group tours by advance reservation.
Admission	Separate fees charged for house and grounds.
Wheelchair access	Most areas.
Special features	Estate restoration; horticultural library; herbarium.

HIGHLAND BOTANICAL PARK
180 Reservoir Avenue   Rochester, NY 14610
(716) 244-8079

Mailing address: Monroe County Department of Parks   375 Westfall Road
Rochester, NY 14620
(716) 274-7750 ∎P ⛲ ⟰ GT ⓘ

Directions	Located south of downtown Rochester; I-490 to Goodman St. exit south; continue to intersection of Goodman St. and Highland Ave.
Hours	Park, every day, dawn to dusk; Lamberton Conservatory, Tuesday, Thursday, Friday, Saturday, and Sunday 10 A.M. to 6 P.M.; Wednesday 10 A.M. to 8 P.M.; closed Monday; extended hours may be scheduled during Lilac Festival and special floral displays; for group tours of park and conservatory, call in advance of visit.
Admission	No fee.
Wheelchair access	Throughout.
Special features	Historic restoration (Warner Castle, headquarters of the Garden Center of Rochester); historic Lamberton Conservatory (visitor center); gifts and refreshments available in the park during Lilac Festival only.

LYNDHURST
635 South Broadway   Tarrytown, NY 10591
(914) 631-0046 ∎P ⟰ ⛪ GT ▣

Directions	Located approximately ½ mi. south of the New York State Thruway (I-87), at the Tappan Zee Bridge on US 9.
Hours	May 2 to October 31 and all of December, Tuesday to Sunday 10 A.M. to 5 P.M.; January to April and all of November, weekends 10 A.M. to 5 P.M.; closed Thanksgiving, Christmas, and New Year's days.
Admission	Fee charged.
Wheelchair access	Throughout, except for the second floor of the mansion; disabled persons requiring additional assistance are encouraged to call for more specific information.
Special features	Historic restoration.

PENNSYLVANIA

BRANDYWINE RIVER MUSEUM
Brandywine Conservancy   P.O. Box 141   Chadds Ford, PA 19317
(215) 388-7601 or (215) 459-1900 ❚P 🝐 ⚐ ✕ 🏠 GT 🅜

Directions	Located on US Rte. 1, near Rte. 100 in Chadds Ford.
Hours	Gardens, open all hours; museum, every day 9:30 A.M. to 4:30 P.M., closed Christmas Day; museum restaurant, open daily 11 A.M. to 3 P.M.
Admission	No fee for gardens; fee charged for museum.
Wheelchair access	Throughout.
Special features	Art gallery/museum.

HENRY FOUNDATION FOR BOTANICAL RESEARCH
P.O. Box 7   801 Stony Lane   Gladwyne, PA 19035
(215) 525-2037 P 🝐 GT ↵

Directions	From Philadelphia, I-76 west to PA-23 west; turn right onto Henry Lane; continue to Stony Lane.
Hours	Tuesday and Thursday 10 A.M. to 4 P.M., April through October; other times and guided tours by appointment.
Admission	No fee.
Wheelchair access	None.

HERSHEY GARDENS
U.S Rte. 422   Hershey, PA 17033
(717) 534-3492 ❚P 🝐 ⚐ ✕ 🏠 GT ⑦ ↵
Mailing address: P.O. Box BB   Hotel Road   Hershey, PA 17033

Directions	Located 90 mi. west of Philadelphia, on Rte. 422, next to Hotel Hershey; Interstate Hwys. 76, 78, 81, and 83 and State Rtes. 39, 322, 422, and 743 all lead to Hershey; follow signs to Hotel Hershey and Hershey Gardens.
Hours	Every day, April through December; April, May, September through December, 9 A.M. to 5 P.M.; Memorial Day through Labor Day, 9 A.M. to 7 P.M.
Admission	Fee charged; no fee for children age 3 and under; special group rate for families of two or more children.
Wheelchair access	Limited.
Special features	Zoo; Hershey Museum of American Life.

LONGWOOD GARDENS
P.O. Box 501   Route 1   Kennett Square, PA 19348-0501
(215) 388-6741 ⬛ P ⊻ ✕ ⅲ GT ⓘ 🎦 ↵

Directions	Located 30 mi. west of Philadelphia, 12 mi. north of Wilmington, Delaware and 3 mi. northeast of Kennett Square, on U.S. 1.
Hours	Every day, April through October, 9 A.M. to 6 P.M.; November through March, 9 A.M. to 5 P.M.; group tours by advance reservation; lighted fountain performances, twice weekly in summer; fireworks performances, monthly in summer (reservations required); organ performances, Sunday at 2:30 P.M., December to April.
Admission	Fee charged; no fee for children age 5 and under.
Wheelchair access	Most areas.
Special features	Estate restoration; lighted fountain performances; fireworks performances; organ performances; outdoor theater and concert presentations.

MEADOWBROOK FARM
1633 Washington Lane   Meadowbrook, PA 19046
(215) 887-5900 ⬛ P ⅲ

Directions	Located approximately 15 mi. north of Philadelphia's city center; I-276 (Pennsylvania Tpke.) to Rte. 611 south; left on Rte. 63 (Welsh Rd.); right on Washington Lane.
Hours	Greenhouse, Monday through Saturday 10 A.M. to 5 P.M.; private garden open during spring and fall to groups of no less than 15 and no more than 35 by advance reservation only.
Admission	No fee.
Wheelchair access	Greenhouse, throughout; private garden, none.
Special features	Commercial greenhouse and nursery.

ARBORETUM OF THE BARNES FOUNDATION
57 Lapsley Lane P.O. Box 128 Merion Station, PA 19066
(215) 664-8880 ∎ ⛾ **GT** ⏎

Directions	Located in the Main Line district west of Philadelphia; Schuylkill Expwy. (I-76) to City Ave. exit; south 2 mi., right at Lapsley La.; from intersection of Rte. 30 and Rte. 1, north 1 mi., left at Lapsley Lane.
Hours	September through June, Monday through Thursday 9:30 A.M. to 4:30 P.M. (entrance at arboretum office, 57 Lapsley Lane); Friday and Saturday 9:30 A.M. to 4:30 P.M. (entrance at 300 N. Latch's Lane); Sunday 1 to 4:30 P.M. (entrance at 300 N. Latch's Lane); July and August, Monday through Friday 9:30 A.M. to 4:30 P.M. (entrance at 57 Lapsley Lane); closed weekends in July and August and all legal holidays; group tours available by advance reservation.
Admission	No fee.
Wheelchair access	Limited.
Special features	Restored estate house containing art school and gallery; write to The Barnes Foundation, Art Gallery, at the above address for visiting policies independent of the arboretum.

BARTRAM'S GARDEN
The John Bartram Association 54th Street and Lindbergh Boulevard
Philadelphia, PA 19143
(215) 729-5281 ∎ **P** ⛾ ⚓ ⅲ **GT** Ⓜ ⏎

Directions	Located on the Schuylkill River, 2 mi. west of downtown Philadelphia.
Hours	Gardens, every day, dawn to dusk; house, May 1 to October 31, Wednesday through Sunday; November 1 to April 31, Wednesday through Friday; noon to 4 P.M. on all days open; group tours, Tuesday through Friday, by advance reservation.
Admission	House, fee charged; garden, no fee.
Wheelchair access	Grounds, most areas; house, limited.
Special features	Historic restoration.

MORRIS ARBORETUM OF THE UNIVERSITY OF PENNSYLVANIA
9414 Meadowbrook Avenue   Philadelphia, PA 19118
(215) 247-5777 (weekdays)   (215) 242-3399 (weekends) ∎ P ♇ GT ⑦ ▣ ♫

Directions	Located about 10 mi. north of the center of Philadelphia, in the Chestnut Hill section, 5 mi. south of the Pennsylvania Tpke. (I-276).
Hours	Weekdays 10 A.M. to 4 to P.M., weekends 10 A.M. to 5 P.M.; guided tours, Saturday and Sunday 2 P.M., from the Hillcrest Ave. entrance.
Admission	Fee charged; no fee for preschoolers.
Wheelchair access	Limited.
Special features	Estate restoration.

THE PENNSYLVANIA HORTICULTURAL SOCIETY
325 Walnut Street   Philadelphia, PA 19106-2777
(215) 625-8250 ∎ ♇ ⅲ ⑦ ▣ ♫

Directions	Located in Independence National Historical Park in old Philadelphia, one block from Independence Hall.
Hours	Every day 9 A.M. to 5 P.M.
Admission	No fee.
Wheelchair access	Throughout.
Special features	Historic restoration; extensive horticultural library; horticultural exhibits.

WYCK
6026 Germantown Avenue   Philadelphia, PA 19144
(215) 848-1690 ∎ ♇ GT ▣

Directions	Located on U.S. 422 (Germantown Ave.) at Walnut Lane in the section known as Germantown, about 6 mi. north of downtown Philadelphia; Schuylkill Expwy. to Johnson St. exit; continue on Johnson St. to Germantown Ave., turn right and travel 4 blocks south to Walnut Lane.
Hours	April 1 through mid-December, Tuesday, Thursday, and Saturday 1 to 4 P.M.; by appointment, year-round, Tuesday through Saturday 9 A.M. to 4 P.M.
Admission	Fee charged.
Wheelchair access	Throughout.
Special features	Historic restoration.

PHIPPS CONSERVATORY
Department of Parks 400 City County Building Pittsburgh, PA 15219
(412) 255-2370 **∎ P ⚲ ⋔ GT**

Directions	Located at the entrance to Schenley Park, on Schenley Dr., in the Oakland section of Pittsburgh, 5 mins. from the city's center.
Hours	Every day 9 A.M. to 5 P.M.; closed Christmas Day and two days before each seasonal flower show.
Admission	Fee charged.
Wheelchair access	Throughout.
Special features	Historic restoration.

PITTSBURGH CIVIC GARDEN CENTER
Mellon Park 1059 Shady Avenue Pittsburgh, PA 15232
(412) 441-4442 **∎ ⚲ ⛆ ⋔ GT ⑦ ▣ ↲**

Directions	Located in Mellon Park, in the Shadyside section of Pittsburgh.
Hours	Grounds, every day, dawn to dusk; gift shop, Monday through Saturday 10 A.M. to 4 P.M.; guided tours by advance reservation; call Monday through Friday 9 A.M. to 4 P.M.
Admission	No fee.
Wheelchair access	Throughout.
Special features	Estate restoration.

SCOTT ARBORETUM
Swarthmore College Swarthmore, PA 19081
(215) 328-8025 **∎ P ⚲ GT**

Directions	Pennsylvania Tpke. to Exit 24 (Valley Forge); two mi. on I-76 to Rte. 320; south 14.5 mi. to College Ave.; turn right and proceed one block to the Scott offices.
Hours	Every day, dawn to dusk.
Admission	No fee.
Wheelchair access	Limited.
Special features	College campus; horticultural library.

RHODE ISLAND

BLITHEWOLD GARDENS & ARBORETUM
Ferry Road   Bristol, RI 02809-0417
(401) 253-2707 ▯▯▯▯▯

Directions	Located midway between Newport and Providence; from Boston, take Rte. 24 to Mt. Hope Bridge exit; cross the Mt. Hope Bridge, bear left at fork onto Ferry Rd. (Rte. 114); Blithewold is ⅛ mi. on the left.
Hours	Grounds, every day 10 A.M. to 4 P.M.; mansion, mid-April to October, 10 A.M. to 4 P.M.; closed Monday and holidays.
Admission	Separate fees for grounds only or mansion-grounds combination; no fee for children age 5 and under.
Wheelchair access	Limited.
Special features	Estate restoration.

NEWPORT MANSIONS
The Preservation Society of Newport County   118 Mill Street   P.O. Box 510 Newport, RI 02840-0939
(401) 847-1000 ▯P▯GT

Directions	Located in the Bellevue section of Newport, with most of the mansions situated along Bellevue Ave.
Hours	Most mansions open every day, May 1 to October 31; Château-sur-Mer, Marble House, and The Elms open weekends during the winter; call for exact hours.
Admission	Fee charged; no fee for children age 5 and under; a variety of group-rate and combination tickets are available; for information and reservations, call (401) 847-6543.
Wheelchair access	Grounds, throughout; interiors are mostly inaccessible, with the exception of The Breakers and Marble House, each equipped with elevators.
Special features	Estate restorations.

GREEN ANIMALS
Cory's Lane   Portsmouth, RI

Mailing address: The Preservation Society of Newport County   118 Mill Street
P.O. Box 510   Newport, RI 02840-0939
(401) 847-1000 ❏ P ⅲ

Directions	Located on Cory's Lane, off State Hwy. 114 (West Main Rd.), 10 mi. north of Newport and 28 mi. south of Providence.
Hours	June 1 through September 30, every day 10 A.M. to 5 P.M.; October, weekends and holidays only, 10 A.M. to 5 P.M.; groups of 20 or more may be admitted at other times by making an appointment with the society; call (401) 847-6543.
Admission	Fee charged; no fee for children age 5 and under; combination tickets for Newport Mansions include Green Animals.
Wheelchair access	Throughout.
Special features	Estate restoration; toy museum; highly recommended, especially for children, is the historic train that takes visitors to Newport, 10 mi. to the south.

ROGER WILLIAMS PARK
Elmwood Avenue   Providence, RI 02905

Mailing address: Department of Public Parks   Providence, RI 02905
(401) 785-9450 ❏ ⚲ ⚓ ✕ ⅲ

Directions	Located approximately 3 mi. south of downtown Providence, near the junction of I-95 and State Hwy. 10.
Hours	Park, every day 7 A.M. to 9 P.M.; hours for specific attractions vary; call for further information.
Admission	Park, no fee; nominal fees for some attractions.
Wheelchair access	Most areas.
Special features	Natural history museum; zoo; planetarium; historic restoration; greenhouses; boathouse.

SHAKESPEARE'S HEAD
Providence Preservation Society   21 Meeting Street   Providence, RI 02903
(401) 831-7440

Directions	Providence is located off I-95 in northeastern Rhode Island; garden is at the intersection of Benefit and Meeting Sts.
Hours	Every day, dawn to dusk.
Admission	No fee.
Wheelchair access	Limited.
Special features	Historic restoration.

WILCOX PARK
71½ High Street   Westerly, RI 02891
(401) 348-8362 ∎P♿⚲GT⟶

Directions	Westerly is on US 1, in southwest Rhode Island; Wilcox Park is located along High, Broad, and Granite Sts. and Grove Ave.
Hours	Every day, dawn to dusk.
Admission	No fee.
Wheelchair access	Throughout.
Special features	Library.

MEADOWBROOK HERB GARDEN
93 Kingstown Road (Rte. 138)   Wyoming, RI 02898
(401) 539-7603 ∎P♿⟶

Directions	Wyoming is located in southeast Rhode Island, about 5 mi. east of the Connecticut border.
Hours	Monday through Saturday 9:30 A.M. to 5 P.M., Sunday 1 to 4 P.M.
Admission	No fee.
Wheelchair access	Throughout.
Special features	Commercial mail-order nursery.

VERMONT

UNIVERSITY OF VERMONT AGRICULTURAL EXPERIMENT STATION
College of Agriculture & Life Sciences   Morrill Hall   Burlington, VT 05405-0106
(802) 656-2980 ∎ P ⬂ ⬛

Directions	Burlington is located in northwestern Vermont, near the New York border; the station is located on Rte. 7 (Pearl St.).
Hours	Summer only, weekdays 8 A.M. to 4 P.M.
Admission	No fee.
Wheelchair access	Throughout.
Special features	University campus.

THE PARK-MCCULLOUGH HOUSE
West Street   P.O. Box 366   North Bennington, VT 05257
(802) 442-5441 ∎ P ⬛ GT

Directions	North Bennington is located on State Hwy. 67 in the southwest corner of Vermont; the house is at the intersection of West and Park Sts.
Hours	House/museum, end of May through end of October, every day 10 A.M. to 4 P.M.; gardens, throughout the year.
Admission	Fee charged for house/museum; no fee for gardens.
Wheelchair access	Gardens, throughout; house/museum, none.
Special features	Historic restoration.

SHELBURNE MUSEUM
Shelburne, VT 05482
(802) 985-3346 ∎ P ✗ ⬛ ⓘ ⬛ ⬛

Directions	Located 7 mi. south of Burlington on Rte. 7.
Hours	Every day, mid-May through October, 9 A.M. to 5 P.M.
Admission	Fee charged.
Wheelchair access	Most areas; wheelchairs available at the Visitor Center.
Special features	Art galleries; a number of historic restorations, including buildings, a sidewheeler ship, and railroad cars; old-fashioned crafts demonstrations and various attractions of special interest to children, including a toy shop and a circus museum.

CANADA

NEWFOUNDLAND

MEMORIAL UNIVERSITY BOTANICAL GARDEN AT OXEN POND
Memorial University of Newfoundland   St. John's, NF A1C 5S7
(709) 737-8590   ⬛P☲GT↩

Directions	The island of Newfoundland lies east of Quebec and north of Nova Scotia; St. John's is located on its eastern coastline; the botanical garden lies adjacent to Pippy Park, on Mt. Scio Rd.
Hours	May 1 to November 30, Wednesday through Sunday 10 A.M. to 5:30 P.M.; guided tours for groups of 10 or more by appointment.
Admission	No fee.
Wheelchair access	Limited.
Special features	University campus.

NOVA SCOTIA

ANNAPOLIS ROYAL HISTORIC GARDENS
P.O. Box 278   Annapolis Royal, NS B0S 1A0
(902) 532-7018   ∎P⛄✕🏠GT ⑦

Directions	The town of Annapolis Royal is located near the Bay of Fundy in southwest Nova Scotia; the gardens are located near the intersection of Prince Albert Rd. (Rte. 1) and Saint George St. (Rte. 8).
Hours	Every day, May through October, 9 A.M. to dusk; restaurant, every day 11 A.M. to 9 P.M.; group tours by advance reservation.
Admission	Fee charged.
Wheelchair access	Throughout.
Special features	Two historic houses; dyke reconstruction.

HALIFAX PUBLIC GARDENS
City of Halifax   Parks & Grounds Division   P.O. Box 812
Armdale, Halifax, NS B3L 4K5
(902) 421-6551   ∎⛄✕

Directions	Located at the intersection of Spring Garden Rd. and South Park St. in downtown Halifax.
Hours	Mid-April to mid-November, every day 8 A.M. to dusk.
Admission	No fee.
Wheelchair access	Throughout.

ONTARIO

DUNDURN CASTLE
Dundurn Park   610 York Boulevard   Hamilton, ON L8R 3H1
(416) 522-5313

WHITEHERN
41 Jackson Street West   Hamilton, ON L8P 1L3
(416) 522-5664 ▉ ▥ **GT**

Directions	Hamilton is on the western shore of Lake Ontario, about 45 mi. south of Toronto; houses located in downtown Hamilton within blocks of each other, Dundurn Castle at intersection of Dundurn St. and York Blvd., Whitehern at intersection of Jackson St. and Bay St.
Hours	Both sites, every day, June 1 to Labour Day (first Monday in September), 11 A.M. to 4 P.M.; Labour Day to May 31, 1 to 4 P.M.; closed Christmas and New Year's days.
Admission	Fee charged for each.
Wheelchair access	Throughout at Dundurn, limited at Whitehern.
Special features	Historic restorations.

GAGE PARK
Department of Public Works   71 Main Street   Hamilton, ON L8N 3T4
(416) 526-4627 **P** ♉ ⚓ **GT**

Directions	Hamilton is located on Lake Ontario, about 45 mi. south of Toronto; park is located in downtown Hamilton, off Main St.
Hours	Park, every day, dawn to dusk; greenhouses, Monday through Friday 8 A.M. to 3 P.M.; first two weeks of November, every day, including weekends, 9 A.M. to 8 P.M.; group tours by advance reservation; children's museum, Tuesday through Saturday 10 A.M. to 4 P.M., Sunday 1 to 4 P.M.; closed Monday, Christmas, Boxing and New Year's days.
Admission	No fee; fee charged for children's museum.
Wheelchair access	Throughout.
Special features	Lawn bowling greens; children's play area; children's museum.

ROYAL BOTANICAL GARDENS
P.O. Box 399   Hamilton, ON L8N 3H8
(416) 527-1158 ▣ P ☕ ✕ ⛫ GT ⑦ ▥ ♬

Directions	Royal Botanical Gardens Centre is located 35 mi. south of Toronto, between the cities of Hamilton and Burlington, at 680 Plains Rd. West (Rte. 2).
Hours	All garden areas, every day, dawn to dusk; group tours by advance reservation.
Admission	Most garden areas, no fee; fee charged for parking at Rock Garden and for indoor Mediterranean Garden.
Wheelchair access	Most areas.
Special features	Children's garden; horticultural library; plant clinic.

NIAGARA PARKS
The Niagara Parks Commission   P.O. Box 150   Niagara Falls, ON L2E 6T2
(416) 356-2241 ▣ P ☕ ✕ ⛫ ⑦

Directions	Queen Victoria Park is located on the Canadian side of the Niagara River, opposite Horseshoe Falls; Floral Clock and Lilac Garden located 7 mi. north, on Niagara Pkwy.
Hours	Queen Victoria Park, Floral Clock, and Lilac Garden, every day, dawn to dusk; Queen Victoria Park Conservatory, July and August 9:30 A.M. to 7 P.M.; all other times, 9:30 A.M. to 4:15 P.M.; during Winter Festival of Lights and holidays, hours are extended; closed Christmas Eve and Christmas Day.
Admission	No fee.
Wheelchair access	Throughout.
Special features	Greco-Roman outdoor theater.

NIAGARA PARKS COMMISSION SCHOOL OF HORTICULTURE
P.O. Box 150   Niagara Falls, ON L2E 6T2
(416) 356-2241 ▣ P ☕ ✕ ⛫ GT ⑦

Directions	Located 5 mi. from the falls, along Niagara Pkwy. North.
Hours	Every day, dawn to dusk.
Admission	No fee.
Wheelchair access	Throughout.
Special features	School of Horticulture campus.

EDWARDS GARDENS AND THE CIVIC GARDEN CENTRE
777 Lawrence Avenue East   North York, ON M3C 1P2
(416) 445-1552 ∎P♀✕ⅲ⑦▥↵

Directions	Located approximately 3 mi. north of Toronto's city center, at the intersection of Lawrence Ave. E. and Leslie St.
Hours	Gardens, every day, dawn to dusk; Garden Centre, weekdays 9:30 A.M. to 4 P.M., weekends 1 to 4 P.M.
Admission	No fee.
Wheelchair access	Throughout.
Special features	Horticultural library.

CENTRAL EXPERIMENTAL FARM
Ottawa Research Station   Building 50   Ottawa, ON K1A 0C6
(613) 995-5222 ∎P♀⚲GT⑦

Directions	Located at the intersection of Preston St. and Carling Ave., approximately 2 mi. south of Ottawa's city center.
Hours	Grounds, every day in summer, dawn to dusk; rest of the year, 8:15 A.M. to dusk; group tours by 1-month advance reservation; guided tours, weekdays 8:30 A.M. to 3:30 P.M.; livestock herds and greenhouse, every day 9 A.M. to 4 P.M.; agricultural museum, every day 9:30 A.M. to 5 P.M.; closed Christmas and New Year's days; wagon ride, first Monday in May through Thanksgiving Day, weekdays 10 to 11:30 A.M. and 2 to 3:30 P.M., weather permitting.
Admission	No fee.
Wheelchair access	Grounds, throughout; buildings, limited.
Special features	Agricultural museum; astronomical observatory.

CULLEN GARDENS AND MINIATURE VILLAGE
300 Taunton Road West   Whitby, ON L1N 5R5
(416) 668-6606 or (416) 294-7965 ∎P♀✕ⅲ

Directions	Located 45 mins. from downtown Toronto; take Hwy. 2 or 401; north on Hwy. 12; left on Taunton Rd. West.
Hours	Every day, mid-April to late April, 10 A.M. to 6 P.M.; late April to mid-May, 9 A.M. to 8 P.M.; mid-May to early September, 9 A.M. to 10 P.M.; early September to early October, 10 A.M. to 8 P.M.; early October to early November, 10 A.M. to 5 P.M.; November 11 through first week in January, 10 A.M. to 10 P.M.; closed Christmas Eve at 5 P.M. and all of Christmas Day.
Admission	Fee charged; no fee for children age 3 and under; group rates for 15 or more by advance reservation.
Wheelchair access	Throughout, except Lynde House.
Special features	Historic restoration; Christmas Festival of Lights.

QUEBEC

METIS GARDENS
Grand Metis, PQ

Mailing address: P.O. Box 242   Mont-Joli, PQ G5H 3L1
(418) 775-2221 ∎ P ✕ ⋔

Directions	Located about 200 mi. northeast of Montreal, on the south bank of the St. Lawrence River, on Rte. 132.
Hours	Every day, June through mid-September, 8:30 A.M. to 8 P.M.
Admission	Gardens, fee charged per automobile; separate fee for Villa Reford, except for children age 7 and under.
Wheelchair access	Limited.
Special features	Estate restoration; museum.

MONTREAL BOTANICAL GARDEN
4101 Sherbrooke Street East   Montreal, PQ H1X 2B2
(514) 872-1400 ∎ P ⛲ ⛟ ✕ ⋔ GT ⑦ 🎦 🔧

Directions	Located opposite the Montreal Olympic Stadium and near Metro Station Pie IX, at the intersection of Rte. 138 (Sherbrooke St.) and Pie IX Blvd.
Hours	Gardens, every day 8 A.M. to dusk; greenhouses, every day 9 A.M. to 6 P.M.; group tours of the greenhouses by advance reservation; call (514) 872-1823.
Admission	Grounds, no fee; fees charged for parking, for greenhouses, for train tour of grounds, and for recorded tour of the greenhouses.
Wheelchair access	Throughout.
Special features	Children's garden.

LIST OF GARDENS

PHOTO CREDITS

All photographs courtesy of the gardens with the exception of those listed below.

INDEX

Page numbers in *italic* indicate illustrations